261
Handcrafts
and Fun

FOR LITTLE ONES

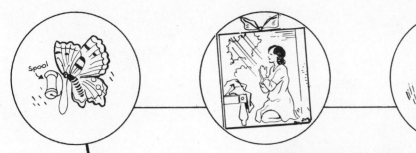

261 Handcrafts and Fun

FOR LITTLE ONES

SIMPLE HANDCRAFTS FOR THE PRE-SCHOOL AND PRIMARY AGES

prepared by ELEANOR DOAN

ZONDERVAN PUBLISHING HOUSE
OF THE ZONDERVAN CORPORATION
GRAND RAPIDS, MICHIGAN 49506

261 HANDCRAFTS AND FUN FOR LITTLE ONES
Copyright 1953 by
Zondervan Publishing House
Grand Rapids, Michigan

Twenty-sixth printing October 1981
ISBN 0-310-23721-1

Printed in the United States of America

261 Answers

Are you looking for simple handcrafts that can be made from scraps and easy-to-find articles?

Here are 261 answers to your problem — some old, some new!

You may also be looking for educational activities rather than pointless entertainment to help the little child become adjusted. Handcraft offers these activities as well as provides an outlet for one of the great drives of human nature: to make something "all my own." It provides therapy for coordination of mind and muscle. With the thrill of achievement come many opportunities to help little people learn to (1) think of others, (2) share, (3) take turns. This teaching can be integrated with the making of every project. Be alert to teaching opportunities and you will find many. Insist upon the completion of one project before another is started.

All craft work needs teacher supervision, and supervision requires preparation. There is essential preparation the teacher must make in following these handcraft projects because pre-school children have not completely coordinated muscular activity and dexterity. The primary children will not need as much help. The success of these projects, therefore, depends upon the teacher, her preparation, and her understanding of children. Of course, none of the objects will be made perfectly! But the children will enjoy the fruit of their efforts, and each achievement brings them closer to success. Encourage and assist the children, but *do not* do the work for them.

THREE SIMPLE RULES will help every craft teacher and parent:
1) Shop early. Keep a supply closet for basic supplies.
2) Prepare in advance — not in class.
3) Encourage and assist children.

Work with the children but let them learn to do *by doing*. See that they finish their work. Let them learn cooperation and citizenship by helping pick up materials, putting away supplies, sharing materials, respecting the rights and property of others. Teach them to conserve supplies and provide clean-up materials such as cloths and paper towels.

The teacher should have a sample of all the handwork which will be made. This serves a dual purpose: the teacher will experience making the object and better anticipate the needs of the pupil, and the child will enjoy seeing what he is going to make and know better how to proceed. Choose those projects which will be enjoyed most by your group, then check your shopping list. Parents should be on the alert for supplies which can be used in making these projects and provide a place to keep them.

USE this book in the
> kindergarten
> Sunday school
> Sunday school extended period
> Vacation Bible School
> weekday activity programs
> home.

You, teacher and parent, will learn 261 answers to happy handcraft accomplishments!

ELEANOR L. DOAN

You will find ...

crafts made from the following articles . . . and crafts listed in some general classifications.

Topical List

OF CRAFTS and FUN

Topical List

OF CRAFTS and FUN

Topical List
OF CRAFTS and FUN

Your Supply Closet

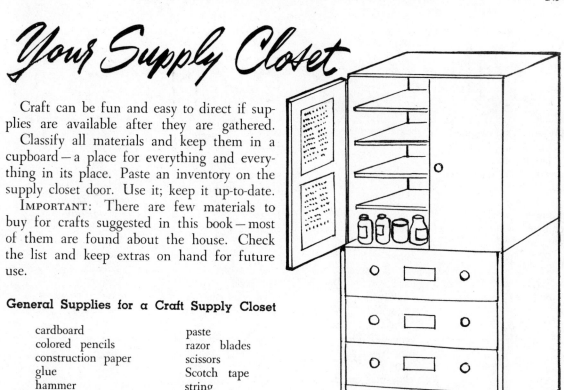

Craft can be fun and easy to direct if supplies are available after they are gathered.

Classify all materials and keep them in a cupboard — a place for everything and everything in its place. Paste an inventory on the supply closet door. Use it; keep it up-to-date.

IMPORTANT: There are few materials to buy for crafts suggested in this book — most of them are found about the house. Check the list and keep extras on hand for future use.

General Supplies for a Craft Supply Closet

cardboard
colored pencils
construction paper
glue
hammer
paper punch
paper towels

paste
razor blades
scissors
Scotch tape
string
thumbtacks
Xacto knife

Supplies to Gather
for making articles in this book

adhesive tape
adhesive tape roll bands
album picture corners
alum, powdered (see recipes)
bags, paper sacks
balls, large and small
bath salts
beads, large, wooden and glass
beans, dried
beets
bells, small
blinds, for scrapbooks
blotter paper, assorted colors
bottles, assorted sizes
bowls, glass
boxes, assorted sizes, cardboard
boxes, small wooden
brads, ½ inch and 1 inch

broom stick
broom straws
brushes
brush bristles
burlap
butcher tape
butter plates, paper
buttons, assorted
calcimine, powder, assorted colors
calendars, assorted sizes, new and old
calico printed scraps
can opener
candy cups
candy papers
candles, assorted sizes
cans, assorted sizes
cardboard
cards, small name
carrots
cellophane paper, assorted colors

cellophane straws
cellophane tape
chalk, white and colored
cheese glasses
chenille wire
Christmas cards
clay
cleaners' garment bags
clothespins, plain and snap varieties
cologne
construction paper, assorted colors
cookie paper cups
cork, large thermos
cork, sheet
corn, dried
cornstarch (see recipes)
corrugated paper, assorted colors
cotton
crayons
crepe paper
cups, paper
decals
dish, large round or square

doilies, paper lace
emery boards
enamel, assorted colors
envelopes, assorted sizes and colors
excelsior
feathers
felt
figurines, inexpensive assorted
finger paint
fingernail polish, colored and plain
flannel scraps
flocking
flour
flower seed
fur scraps
furniture cups, rubber
garment bags from cleaners
garden flowers, fresh
gelatin (see recipes)
gingham scraps
glasses
glitter, assorted colors
gloves, clean cotton, white and colored

Your Supply Closet

glue
glycerin (see recipes)
graph paper, for enlarging patterns
greeting cards, assorted
gum, chewing
gumdrops
gummed paper hangers
gummed reinforcements
gummed seals: flowers, stars, etc.
hairpins
ice cream cartons, large and small
jar lids
jar rubbers
jars, assorted sizes
lace
lace doilies, paper
lollipops
mailing tubes, assorted sizes
milk bottle caps
milk bottles, cardboard
mirrors
muslin scraps
nails
nail polish, colored and plain
needles, assorted
newspapers
newsprint paper
oil of wintergreen (see finger paint)
oilcloth
paints, water colors
pans, large round or square
paper bats
paper cups, assorted
paper cups, cornucopia style
paper doilies
paper note pads
paper plates, large and small
paper straws
paper towels
paraffin
passe partout picture binding
paste
pencils, lead and colored

pictures: animals, children, Christmas scenes, flowers, butterflies, sailors, people, Jesus, sacred subjects
pinecones
pins, straight and safety
plaster, patching
popcorn cans
potatoes, sweet
raffia
reinforcements, gummed
ribbon scraps
rickrack braid
rings from adhesive tape rolls
rocks, small pretty ones
rubber balls, small
rubber bands
sachets
safety pins
salt (see recipes)
salt and pepper shakers
sand, strained
sandpaper
scissors, blunt
scrapbooks
screen, window
sea shells
seaweed, dried
seed catalogs
seed pods, dried
seeds, bean, squash, nasturtium, pansy
shelf paper
shellac
shoestrings
soap flakes (see finger paint)
soap, white toilet and ivory
spice boxes, empty
spools, assorted
spoons
starfish
starch, laundry (see recipes)
stars, gummed
sticks, narrow and 10 or 12 inches long
stockings, white cotton

straws, paper
string
sucker sticks
tacks, assorted
talcum
tape, adhesive and cellophane
thread
thumbtacks
tile
tissue paper, colored and white
toothpicks, colored
trimz wallpaper borders
tubes, mailing
turnips
turtles, small live ones
twigs and branches
twine
vegetable coloring, assorted colors

wallpaper, assorted
wallpaper borders
wax paper
weeds, pretty dried ones
window blinds
window screen
wire, chenille
wire, plain
witch hazel
wood, sticks ruler size
wooden spoons and forks
wrapping paper
yarn scraps

BOTTLES AND JARS

Bottles and jars! Cupboards and medicine cabinets are full of them. Round up all the attractive jars and bottles and select those that can be used for these craft projects. Discard the rest. Let the children help you wash and dry the bottles. Remember to win the child's confidence and love as you work with him.

BOTTLES AND JARS
(*Also see* CORRUGATED CRAFT,
RAFFIA *and* DECALS.)

PAPERWEIGHTS

Choose a small marmalade, maraschino cherry, or mustard jar, with lid; some white sand, several colors of chalk and paper toweling.

Select several sticks of colored chalk and make into dust by rubbing on paper toweling. Mix each color with sand until colored. Pour colored sand, layer upon layer, into jar or bottle until filled. Seal with lid. The child will enjoy finishing his paperweight by applying a small decal to the top of the lid or on the side of the jar. One of these will be appreciated by father for his desk.

FLOWER SEED HOLDERS

Select several small jars or olive bottles the same size, with lids; pictures of flowers from seed catalogs or magazines: daisies, cosmos, larkspur, marigolds, etc.

Children may wash and dry the jars or bottles, then cut out the pictures of flowers. Glue one picture to the top or on the side of a jar. These little holders will make excellent seed sorters when mother gathers seed at the end of the summer. Also, this project will help the child to know how God plans for us to have flowers and how He helps the flowers to give us the seeds.

COTTON PICKER

Materials needed: little jar without a screw lid, a cardboard disc the size of the jar opening, a six-inch square of white or pink crepe paper, cotton balls to fill the jar plus a little extra for stuffing the doll head, two strips of colored crepe paper about 4 and 6 inches wide and about 24 inches long (depending upon size of jar), thread, crayons, adhesive tape, glue, piece of ribbon.

Make a cotton ball from the extra bit of cotton and place in the center of a six-inch paper square. Tie to make head. Use crayon to color face. Paste head on cardboard disc. Gather paper strip (four-inch width) around neck of doll and tie in place with ribbon. Fasten six-inch width piece of crepe paper around jar for skirt. The teacher may help the child to fasten the doll to the jar by making a hinge of adhesive tape from cardboard to jar. Place cotton balls in jar. Lift doll by head and reach into jar for cotton.

COIN AND BUTTON BANKS

Save unusual-shaped jars with tight-fitting lids. Bits of adhesive tape, decals or colored fingernail polish will finish these projects.

Have slits cut in the jar tops ¼ inch wide and 1¼ inch long. Press the metal back so little hands cannot be hurt. Line jar tops with cardboard (cutting slit to match top) or cover edges of slits with adhesive tape. Decals may be pressed onto the jars or the child can paint designs with colored fingernail polish. Completed jars may be used for banks or for mother's buttons. Make a bank for each member of the family for penny-a-meal offerings, etc.

DOOR STOPS

For this project save quart milk bottles or large, unusual-shaped bottles or jars, colored chalk, white sand, paper toweling or sandpaper.

The child may prepare colored sand by mixing chalk dust with sand. (To obtain chalk dust, rub the chalk on paper toweling or sand paper.) Put sand in the bottle or jar in colored layers to give a marble effect. Help the child seal with paraffin or a tight fitting cap.

Door stops may also be made for use in the Sunday school. This will help the child to learn that he can help to make God's house more attractive.

RATTLES

Gather: small, attractive wide-mouth bottles such as Alka-Seltzer or olive bottles, colored wooden beads, dried corn or beans, a tight-fitting bottle cap for each bottle, adhesive tape, ribbon or yarn.

Wash bottles, remove labels, dry bottles and caps. The child may place colored beads or dried corn or beans (or small trinkets)

in each bottle. After he screws the lid on each bottle, help him seal it with adhesive tape and tie on a gay yarn or ribbon bow. (Plastic bottles make good rattles, too.)

One of these rattles will make a fine gift for baby brother or sister or a wee relative. Or, rattles can be made for the Cradle Roll and Nursery Departments of the Sunday school. The preparing and giving of gifts helps the pre-school child learn to share and to think of others.

BOTTLE GIFTS

Save and wash all unusual bottles or jars with lids. Wash and remove labels. Help the child decorate these with decals or with colored fingernail polish. They may be used to hold bath salts for sister, herbs for mother, nails and screws for father, marbles for brother.

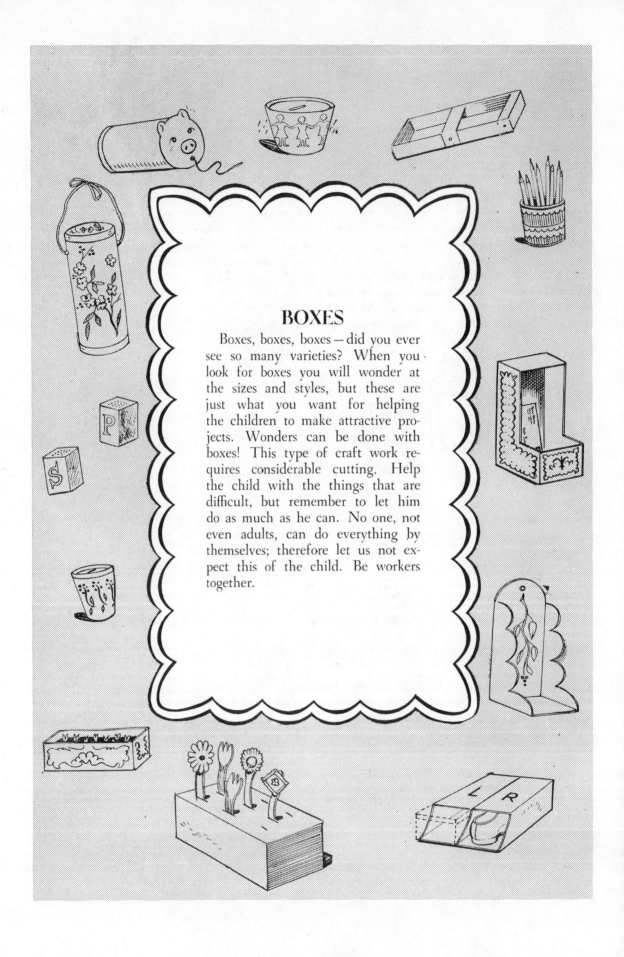

BOXES

Boxes, boxes, boxes — did you ever see so many varieties? When you look for boxes you will wonder at the sizes and styles, but these are just what you want for helping the children to make attractive projects. Wonders can be done with boxes! This type of craft work requires considerable cutting. Help the child with the things that are difficult, but remember to let him do as much as he can. No one, not even adults, can do everything by themselves; therefore let us not expect this of the child. Be workers together.

BOXES
(Also see GAMES, CORRUGATED
CRAFT *and* TOYS.)

FLOWER BED

Provide each child with the bottom part of a square box. (An oblong one will do, too.) Cut slits on top of box with razor blade. Then let child color box green on the sides and brown on top. You will need a supply of wooden picnic spoons and forks. The children may color the forks like tulips, making the handles green for stems. Provide seed catalogs and magazines with flower pictures. The children may cut out flowers and paste them on the backs of the spoons. Gummed flower seals may be used also. Candy cups or small butter plates may be pasted on the spoons for variety in flowers. After all stems are colored green, insert flowers in the flower bed. Talk about the lovely flowers God made for us to enjoy.

WHATNOT

A shoe box is best for this little shelf. Sketch design on the box and cut out for child. He may color shelf brown and paste on some design cut from a magazine or wallpaper. Punch a hole in the whatnot for hanging, or attach loop of string on back with Scotch tape.

Encourage children to make some of these shelves for their Sunday school rooms.

Fork tulip

Spoon Daisy

Candy Paper Flower

Butter Plate Flower

Shoes

WHAT NOT

LETTER HOLDERS

(1) Select a cereal box. Trace pattern for child with heavy crayon marks. Let child cut out design. Provide blunt-end scissors. The child may cover the holder with wallpaper. This handy holder will be a highly acceptable gift for father to use on his desk or for mother to keep in the kitchen for her shopping list, coupons, recipes, etc.

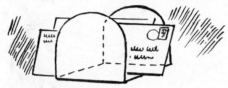

(2) Select a box with four sides as intact as possible — such as a cracker box. Sketch design for cutting and let child do this if he can. Seal any open ends together to close box. Child may cover the holder with greeting cards, wallpaper, or finger paint.

SPICE HOLDER

This is an easy cutting job for the child. Choose any box 12 or more inches long. Cut as noted in sketch. Cover outside of shelf with finger paint or wallpaper, and line inside with white shelf paper. Mother would be happy for one or more of these holders in her cupbord. These would also be welcomed by Sunday school teachers. Crayons could be kept in such a holder after being placed in small baby food cans.

LEAVE-A-NOTE HOLDER

A butter carton or similar box is fine for this project. Cut as noted. Color box if it is not coated with a wax finish, otherwise cover with wallpaper or gingham. Place a pad of paper and a pencil in box. Tie a string to pencil then punch a hole in the box and fasten string through hole. Thumbtack holder near door. Now visitors can write a note when family is away. This would be a fine gift for every Sunday school room, too! Encourage child to help make improvements in God's house with such gifts.

This same box design may be used for
1) Brush holder for closets.
2) Grocery shopping list for kitchen.
3) Key holder. (Use a smaller box.)
4) Father's receipts.

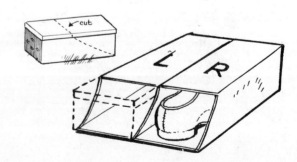

SHOE HOLDERS

Let children help gather boxes, two the same size for each child. Cut box and lid as noted in sketch, then paste lid to box. Use a brad to fasten boxes together after pasting them together. Color or cover boxes with gingham. Help child draw or cut out and paste on the letters "L" (for left) and "R" (for right) on boxes. Right and left shoes can then be placed in the correct places. If possible, use children's size shoe boxes. Parents will welcome the making of this project to help the child keep his closet neat and to help the child f.nd the correct shoes quickly.

BOAT

Use a cardboard milk carton (square style) and cut in half, lengthwise, allowing for the middle strip and end piece as noted in sketch. Fold end piece to form seat and fasten to sides with paper brads. Fasten center strip with brad to form seat. Wax on carton will cause boat to float. Children may cut out figures of sailors or people to place in boat.

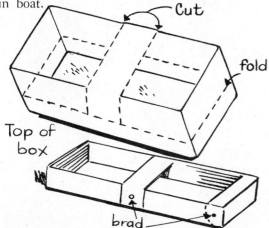

SUGAR, SALT AND PEPPER SHAKERS

Select two small and one large cream cartons. (Other boxes with lids will do as well.) Cover boxes with paper, or color with *wax* crayons. (Wax crayons will blend into wax on cartons.) Punch holes in the tops of the boxes with nails (large for sugar shaker, medium for salt, and small for pepper). Fasten tops securely after filling boxes. These are handy for picnic or patio use.

WINDOW BOXES

Use a one or two quart milk carton and cut away one side. Color or cover with gingham or gift-wrap paper (sides and ends only). Place a few pebbles in box, then fill with soil. Child will enjoy making this and then will enjoy planting nasturtium or pansy seeds. Or, transplant small geraniums into

box. Window boxes such as this one will brighten up Sunday school rooms as well as the home. Also, they will help the child to think about making God's house beautiful. Talk about how God plans for flowers to grow. Remind the child of God's greatness every time the plants are watered.

EGG CARTON HANDIES

By removing one or more divisions in an egg carton, and the top, many uses can be found for the box. A series of these handy boxes can be decorated attractively by the child.

1) DESK SORTER

Remove four divisions and make an acceptable gift for father where he can keep stamps, paper clips, thumbtacks, pencils, etc.

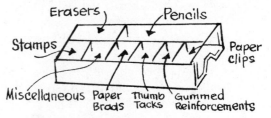

2) WORKSHOP SORTER

Without removing the partitions, use the box for separating screws, nails, bolts, etc.

3) MOTHER'S SEWING SORTER

Remove one partition to accommodate a tape measure. Use remaining divisions for thread, pins, needles, thimble, etc.

4) SOX BOX

Remove every other partition on both sides of carton and the spaces will provide room for the child's sox. The use of this helps the child to sort and roll sox together and keep them neat and where they can be found easily.

5) PLANTERS

Place a dozen little paper cups, filled with soil, in the divisions of the carton. Let children plant seeds in these containers then watch little plants grow. Keep planters in windows. They will make any Sunday school room attractive.

BANKS

Use an ice cream or cottage cheese carton with lid sealed on. Child may color or decorate as he chooses. Cut slot in top of box for him.

Child may cut paper dolls (see *Paper Cutting and Folding*) the height of the bank, and color them red, yellow, black and brown. Faces may be drawn in. Paste dolls around bank. This will be a fine reminder for missionary giving.

PIGGY STRING HOLDER

Use a salt box or round cereal box for this project. Save string and let child roll it into a large, continuous ball that will fit into the box. Cut out a pig's head from cardboard and color. (Enlarge design as suggested below.) Paste head on box top. Cut hole for mouth, through which string will feed. Feed string into mouth and paste lid on box. Child may color box. This holder makes an ideal gift to all the family and will help the child to be thrifty in saving string.

PENCIL AND BRUSH HOLDERS

Assorted sizes of round boxes make gay brush or pencil holders. Cover with colored paper or muslin. Decorate by pasting on colored cutouts or by using odds and ends of rickrack braid.

KNITTING AND MENDING BOXES

A round box, a shoestring, some colored paper and flowers cut from magazines make a handy box for mother. Cover box with colored paper and paste colored flowers, etc., on for a design. Color lid of box and attach to box with adhesive or masking tape so it will not become lost. Punch a hole in each side of the box. Cut shoestring in half and attach to box. Or, to keep the box from tearing, tie a knot in the cut end of the shoestring, run a large bead or button on the string and then run the string through the box hole. Add another bead or button and tie a knot. Tie shoestring ends together for handle. Children may make attractive boxes by covering them with cretonne.

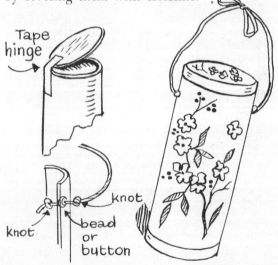

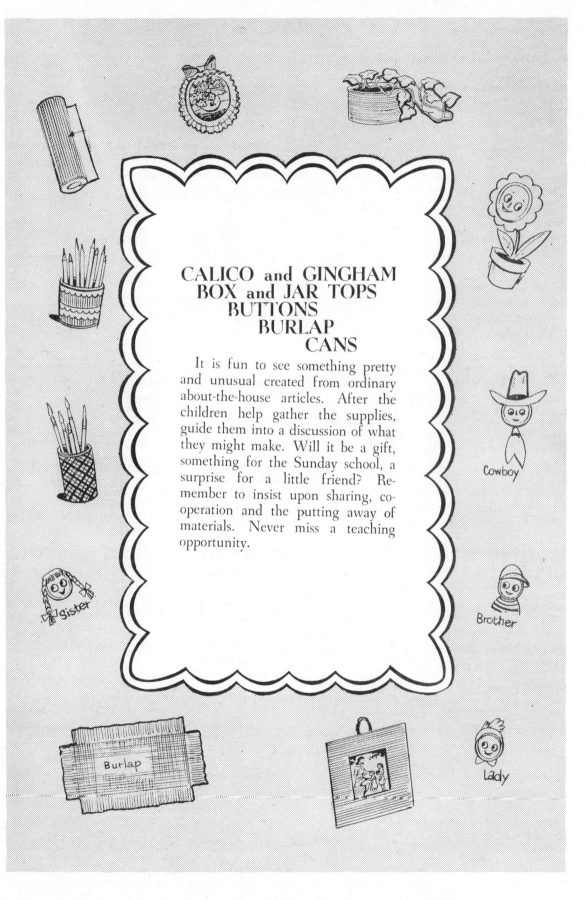

CALICO and GINGHAM
BOX and JAR TOPS
BUTTONS
BURLAP
CANS

It is fun to see something pretty and unusual created from ordinary about-the-house articles. After the children help gather the supplies, guide them into a discussion of what they might make. Will it be a gift, something for the Sunday school, a surprise for a little friend? Remember to insist upon sharing, co-operation and the putting away of materials. Never miss a teaching opportunity.

Cowboy

Sister

Brother

Burlap

Lady

CALICO AND GINGHAM CRAFT

CALICO AND GINGHAM PICTURES

Provide outline pictures of children, or let child draw pictures. Also provide rick-rack braid, vegetable glue, scraps of gingham and calico, cardboard and yarn.

Help child cut out gingham or calico to fit outline of clothing in picture child has drawn. Cover back of gingham with vegetable glue. Place cloth on picture and smooth out wrinkles. Place under weight to dry. Paste picture on cardboard and make a border by pasting rickrack tape around edges. Help child punch holes and let him put yarn through holes, and tie, for hanger.

ALTERNATE SUGGESTION

Help child cut out clothing such as dresses, overalls, etc. He may paste this on cardboard and then draw head, arms and legs with crayons. The child will love to create all sorts of little calico friends. Perhaps he can make the gingham dog and the calico cat!

CANS

There is great teaching value in planning, and by letting the children assist you, much more can be accomplished than you would believe possible. Let the little folk sort cans, remove paper labels then wash cans. The projects suggested will be useful in the Sunday school as well as in the home and kindergarten. A personal interest in helping make God's house attractive cannot start too early in life.

CAN CRAFT

Save assorted sizes of cans: from baby food, coffee, fruits, brown breads, etc. Be certain that the lids are cut off smoothly and with a can opener that leaves a finished rolled edge. Provide a supply of decals, colored corrugated paper, raffia, glue, oilcloth strips and paste.

1) VASES

Use the tall cans and remove the paper. Cut corrugated to fit can and glue on. Or, cover can with twisted raffia. (See index, *Raffia*.)

Corrugated

2) CRAYON HOLDERS

Enamel the baby food cans in advance of time needed. Or let the children paste strips of colored oilcloth around cans. Decals may be applied. Use one can for each color of crayon — the matching color if possible.

Red   Blue   Green

3) PLANTERS

Use the one-pound size coffee cans for planters. Cover cans with oilcloth, corrugated, or raffia. Apply decals if oilcloth is used. Place a few small rocks in bottom of cans if plants are to be placed directly in them; otherwise put the plants in pottery containers and then place in cans.

Raffia

BOX AND JAR TOPS
(*Also see* RAFFIA.)

WALL PICTURES

Box tops from round cereal boxes may be made into several styles of pictures. Holes may be punched and ribbon or yarn used for a hanger. Several pictures may be fastened together.

1) SPRING PICTURES

Cut designs from greeting cards or magazines and paste to strip of paper folded into a spring. Paste spring to center of box top after it has been colored.

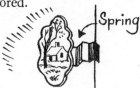

2) SHADOW PICTURE

Choose a picture to paste into box top. Color outer edge of box top and add a ruffle of crepe paper or lace.

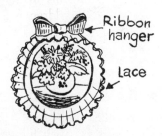

3) THIRD-DIMENSION PICTURE

Use a fluted candy or cookie paper cup and fold in half by creasing bottom and sides. Paste it into box top with bottom fitting lower contour of box to form a "basket." Gather dried weeds or flowers and paste into paper "basket." Or, flowers may be cut from periodicals and pasted into "basket."

COASTERS

There are many box and jar tops that would make coasters for glasses, vases, or small potted plants. Pictures may be pasted in the center of the cardboard box tops if they are to be used for glasses. Circles may be cut from oilcloth to fit the jar and box tops if these are to be made into coasters for vases or potted plants.

BURLAP

PLACE MATS

Provide squares of burlap 9 x 12 inches, two for each child. Pull a thread on each side, one inch from edge, then let child pull threads up to that place to make fringe. Fringe may be colored with large crayons. These mats make lovely gifts for mother.

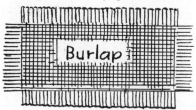

BURLAP PICTURES

Provide prints of sacred pictures, pieces of cardboard and burlap the same size. Let child cover one side of cardboard with paste and press burlap onto it. Cover back of picture with paste and press over burlap. Place a piece of white paper over picture and rub firmly for a few minutes. The burlap will cause the picture to look like an oil painting. Bind picture with colored cellophane tape. Paste a loop of string on back with tape for hanger.

BUTTONS

Button, button, who has a button? Gather large and small two-hole buttons, bits of feathers, cardboard, crayons, a pencil and some glue. See what fun the children will have making faces, people, animals and flowers. Encourage them to make the faces of Bible people or a scene from a Bible story where there are several people.

FLOWERS

Paste buttons on cardboard. Draw petals around button. Add a stem, leaves and a flower pot. Then draw a flower face on the button with pencil or crayon.

PEOPLE AND ANIMALS

Several people and animals can be drawn on a piece of cardboard. Use buttons for faces and glue in place. Draw a little girl, a little boy, a kitten or a rooster. Glue a few feathers to the rooster to make him look real. Remember, teacher, let the child do the work.

Use the same idea and encourage the children to draw Bible people. Perhaps they could make the figures of the children who went to see Jesus.

FACES

There are many faces you can make with buttons. Perhaps you can make the faces of your family or of your playmates. Children will enjoy thinking of whom they will picture. Help them add a bit of cloth for a hat or collar, rope for hair, or a feather in a hat for a touch-and-feel effect. If the faces are made on cardboard they can be bound with colored cellophane tape and a gummed hanger can be added so that the "picture" can be hung on the wall.

BUTTON PLACE CARDS AND GIFT TAGS

Provide the child with small cards size 3 x 2½ inches (a 3 x 5 inch file card cut in half). Let him choose what he wishes to make with buttons.

Button faces on the place cards will be welcomed by mother, especially if they are personalized for the guests. Name the faces and add braided yarn or a bit of cotton colored with water colors for hair. (The teacher may color the cotton beforehand.) The child may make his own place cards for his own guests.

CLOTHESPINS – CORK

These crafts are simple and offer the child enjoyment of accomplishing something by himself. Remember to encourage him. Do not expect finished products to look adult-made. Let the child tell you about his plans for using these projects and use his answers for teaching opportunities.

CLOTHESPIN CRAFT

NAPKIN HOLDERS

1) Pinch clothespin (with spring)
2) Wooden clothespin (no spring)

Paint clothespin with enamel or dip in vegetable coloring diluted with water. Help child write his name then trace it on clothespin. Child may make a different colored holder for each member of the family and a few extra ones for guests.

STAND-UP ANIMALS

Provide two clothespins for each four-legged animal and one clothespin for each bird. The spring type clothespins are required. Also provide crayons, vegetable coloring, drawing paper and construction paper.

Enlarge patterns on drawing paper as suggested below and trace on construction paper. Children may color and cut out bodies of animals and birds. Dip clothespins in vegetable dye and allow to dry. When bodies are completed and the clothespins dry, children may clip clothespins onto bodies for legs. Stand animals and birds up on table. An assortment of these will be helpful in telling the story of Noah and the Ark.

flamingo

NOTEBOARD

You will need the following materials:

Piece of corrugated cardboard 24 x 15 inches

Butcher tape, 2-inch width

Clothespins, one for each member of family

Tacks for posting the board (or wire for hanging)

Help children bind the cardboard with the butcher tape. Add a wallpaper border (Trimz) if desired. Color the clothespins (with crayons or dip in diluted vegetable coloring) a different color for each member of the family. Hang or tack board in kitchen, hall, or near the telephone, at height children can reach. Clip all notes or memos for members of the family with their respective clothespins. The rest of the board may be used as a tack board.

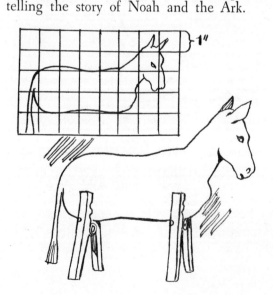

CORK CRAFT

SANDALS

Provide the following for each child: wrapping paper, pencil, two shoelaces (or heavy waxed twine) and sheet-cork, sufficient for two shoe soles.

Trace both feet on wrapping paper. Paste pattern lightly on cork and cut out. Remove pattern. Punch four holes as noted in illustration, using punch or a large nail. Insert shoe laces and the sandals are ready to wear.

Perhaps these sandals are like the ones Jesus wore, or similar to those worn by the children who went to see Jesus. Teacher, you might let the children wear the sandals and gather about you to hear a favorite Bible story.

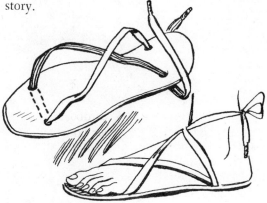

COASTERS

For each coaster you will need a three-inch diameter of cork, bits of colored paper for the doily design or greeting card flowers for other designs, glue, shellac and brush.

Cut doily design (See *Paper Cutting and Folding*) and paste to cork. Or, cut flowers from greeting cards and paste to cork. When dry shellac the coasters. Make a set of four.

HOT PLATE MATS

1) DOILY DESIGN

Provide: a 7-inch square of colored paper, 7½-inch square of cork, glue, scissors, shellac, brush for shellac.

Cut doily by folding paper in half and then in half again. Fold a third time and cut. Scallop the edge and cut any design desired. Open and glue to cork. Place upside down on wax paper (so as not to stick to papers) and weight down. When dry shellac. Trim corners of cork diagonally if desired.

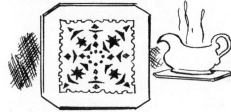

2) FLOWER DESIGN

Provide: a 10-inch oval of cork, small pieces of colored construction paper, shellac and brush, scissors and glue.

Select a flower design easy to cut on folded sheets. (Note illustration.) Cut out design and glue to cork. After glue is dry, shellac mat.

stem   flower   pot

CORK BOATS

Provide each child with a large cork, a toothpick (plastic ones are best) and a 2-inch square of white paper cut diagonally in two. Insert toothpick through paper sail and stick one end in cork. Provide pan of water and let children sail their boats. Write owner's name on sail of each boat.

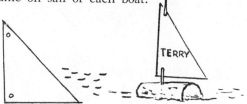

TERRY

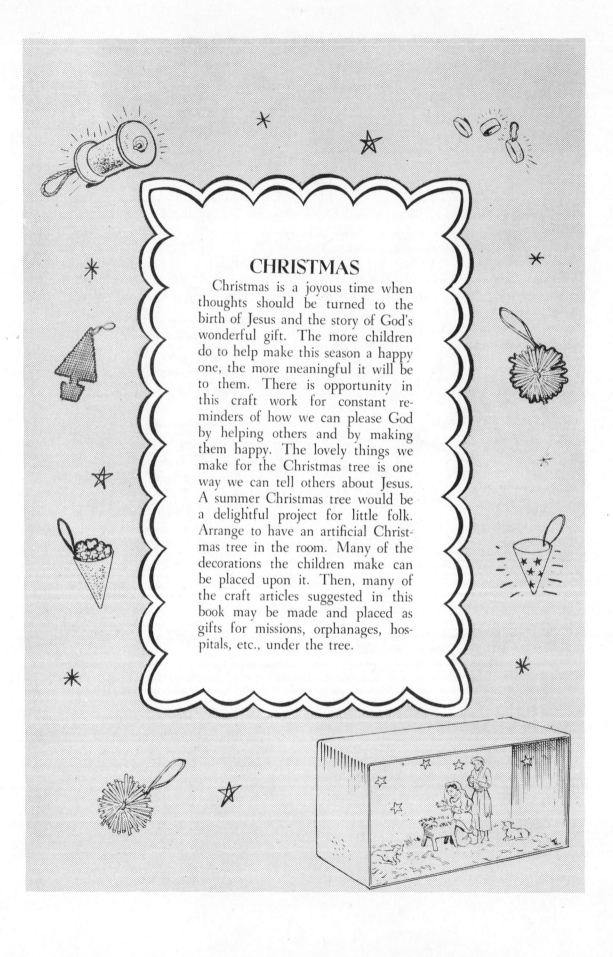

CHRISTMAS

Christmas is a joyous time when thoughts should be turned to the birth of Jesus and the story of God's wonderful gift. The more children do to help make this season a happy one, the more meaningful it will be to them. There is opportunity in this craft work for constant reminders of how we can please God by helping others and by making them happy. The lovely things we make for the Christmas tree is one way we can tell others about Jesus. A summer Christmas tree would be a delightful project for little folk. Arrange to have an artificial Christmas tree in the room. Many of the decorations the children make can be placed upon it. Then, many of the craft articles suggested in this book may be made and placed as gifts for missions, orphanages, hospitals, etc., under the tree.

CRAFTS FOR CHRISTMAS

(Also see Paper Cups *for bells,*
Mailing Tubes, Recipes *and*
Spools *for ornaments.)*

POM-POMS

Also see *Paper Straws.*

Select ten colored cellophane straws. Cut in half. Tie together in center with gift wrap ribbon and hang on Christmas tree.

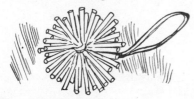

SCREEN ORNAMENTS

Gather odds and ends of new wire screen. Trace patterns of star, tree, bell, etc., on screen with chalk. Cut out designs for children. Provide yarn or string and large needles and let children overcast edges of screen ornaments. Be sure to obtain the blunt-end needles. Cover ornaments with thin film of paste and sprinkle with glitter.

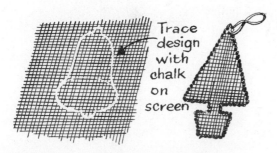

Trace design with chalk on screen

CHRISTMAS CANDLE HOLDERS

Each child will need two large and two small spools. Wash spools and dye them green by dipping them into diluted green vegetable coloring. Glue small spools on top of large ones. Cut circles from red paper and paste holders on circle. Put small red candles in the spool holders. Place a candle at each side of the manger scene.

POPCORN CORNUCOPIAS

Gather some paper cups, paste, gummed stars, ribbon and glitter. Decorate cups with stars or cover with paste and sprinkle on some glitter. Tie a ribbon through a hole punched with pencil and hang on tree. Fill with popcorn.

SPOOL BELLS

Wash spools and dip in vegetable coloring that has been diluted with water. String each spool on colored yarn and fasten a bead at one end of spool for clapper. (See sketch.) Spool bells may be made with plain spools covered with paste then sprinkled with glitter.

GLITTER RINGS

Cut circles of varying width from mailing tubes. Cover with paste and sprinkle with glitter. String on yarn or ribbon and hang on tree.

MANGER SCENE

Provide a shoe box for each child, gummed stars, excelsior, cotton, pictures of sheep, Mary and Joseph and the Christ Child in the manger (cut from Christmas cards). Cut away half of one side of the box for each child. The child may paste gummed stars in the back (or bottom) of box. He then may cut out the manger scene and paste in back of box. Cover bottom of manger scene (side on which box rests) with excelsior after it has been covered with a thin film of paste.

Child may cut out sheep and cover with paste. Add bits of cotton for wool and stand sheep in straw (excelsior) near manger.

The manger scene may be used for the family's worship service on Christmas day. It may also be used in Sunday school or as a visual aid whenever the story of Baby Jesus is told.

CORRUGATED PAPER CRAFT

Many attractive gifts and projects can be made from this about-the-house material. The items suggested here are quite simple for the little child to make and will help him to see how useful ordinary materials can be. It will spur his own creativeness.

Help the little child to follow instructions, take turns using supplies and putting away equipment. Help him to plan gifts and talk over the ideas he may have for varying the projects. Help him to thank God for his teachers and those who love him and want to assist him.

CORRUGATED PAPER CRAFT
(Also see CORK CRAFT *and* CANS.*)*

Corrugated paper may be purchased in small rolls. It is available in many colors and is sometimes marked on the plain side in inch squares for cutting. Flexible packing corrugated paper is also recommended if it is not crushed.

VASES

Select glasses, jars or bottles for vases. Cut a piece of corrugated cardboard to fit around each vase, with ribbing running up and down. Cover cardboard with glue and fasten to container. Scotch tape may be used to protect seam. Child may color paper if plain color is used.

PLANTERS

Use a large can (2½ size tin or coffee can) and cover with a strip of corrugated paper cut to fit. Encourage child to choose attractive color combinations in coloring. Contrasting colors of paper may be used. Put a few small rocks in the can before adding soil and plant.

INK BOTTLES, PENCIL HOLDER, WASTEBASKET

Make a gift for father. Small strips of corrugated paper can be glued around an ink bottle. A glass can be covered to match the bottle for holding pencils. Perhaps a popcorn can or large ice cream carton can be covered for a wastebasket.

PICTURE FRAMES

Provide scissors, glue, picture, corrugated (natural or colored), plain cardboard, yarn or string.

Mark the size of the picture to be framed on corrugated paper. Adult may assist child in cutting an opening and removing this square of paper. Mount picture on piece of cardboard the same size as the frame. Place loop of yarn or string on cardboard to form hanger. Glue corrugated frame on cardboard, allowing hanger to extend out about one inch.

FISH

White and colored corrugated cardboard scraps are needed for this project. Also provide a pencil, string, crayon, glue and blunt-end scissors.

Cut two circles of equal size, four inches in diameter or larger, one from corrugated and one from plain cardboard. Contrasting or harmonizing colors may be used. Cut corrugated circle in half with ribbing going horizontally. Cut one of these half circles in half again. Use the half circle for the tail and the remaining pieces for fins. Paste these on the back of the plain cardboard circles. Draw an eye and mouth. Attach string to back with Scotch tape and hang fish about room. Make some white fish and some colored fish.

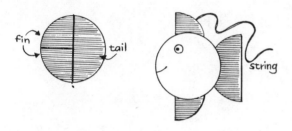

AQUARIUM

Make fish as described above in assorted sizes. Obtain a corrugated box, cut off flaps and turn with opening on side. Crumple blue paper in bottom of box for water. Attach fish, by string, to top of box with glue or Scotch tape. If possible, cover box opening with sheet of blue cellophane. Use one of these aquariums in Sunday school when telling the story of God's creation of the sea and the fish.

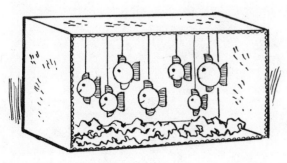

PENCIL OR BRUSH HOLDER

Cut strips of colored corrugated paper about 3 inches wide and 30 inches long. The ribbing should run parallel with the 3-inch width. Roll up strip and fasten end with Scotch tape. Tie ribbon or yarn around the center of the roll. Add a few gummed seals. This will make a handy holder for pencils or brushes. Keep one in the kitchen, another near the telephone and one in the workshop. Sunday school teachers and secretaries would like to have some of these, too.

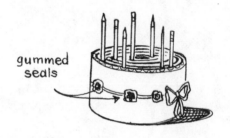

CROWNS

Use corrugated paper with ribbing running widthwise. Cut any design desired for a crown and if possible, let children do the cutting. Cut cardboard patterns and trace on corrugated paper with heavy crayons. The corrugated side should be worn on the outside. Child may color crowns, decorate with gummed stars, or cover with film of paste and sprinkle on some glitter. Measure crown on child's head and fasten with Scotch tape.

COTTON – DECALS

Every little child expresses the desire to "do it by myself." These crafts can be made by 4-to-6 year-olds without much assistance. They will enjoy planning the use of projects or making of gifts. Several items offer opportunities for reviewing Bible stories or making an application. Let the child do the talking about his work and the stories that come to mind. Being a good listener is one-half of being a good conversationalist.

COTTON

WOOLLY SHEEP

Make the fuzzy sheep from chenille wire and cotton. Pinch off a piece of cotton about 2 x 1 inches for sheep and two lengths of chenille wire 2½ inches long for legs. Twist one piece of wire around cotton, about ¾ inch from end, to form head and front feet. Twist second piece of wire about ¼ inch from opposite end to form tail and back legs. Arrange wire legs so sheep will stand.

Use a shoe box, without lid, and cut an opening for a door into a sheepfold. Review stories of the Little Lost Sheep, the Good Shepherd, etc.

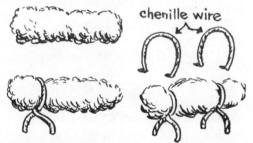

chenille wire

FLUFFY CHICK

For a little chick provide cotton, a cardboard circle 4 inches in diameter, paste, yellow chalk or calcimine powder, excelsior, thread, sandpaper or paper toweling and scraps of yellow and black paper.

Make yellow chalk dust by rubbing yellow chalk on paper toweling or sandpaper. Children may make a ball of cotton and rub it in the chalk dust until it is yellow. Shape cotton into an oblong ball and tie off head section with thread. Cut three yellow double triangles for feet and mouth. Paste in place. Add two black paper dots for eyes. (Make these with a paper punch if you have one.) Cover cardboard disc with paste and sprinkle on excelsior. Paste chick in the center of the cardboard.

fold

excelsior

feet and mouth pattern

PUSSY WILLOWS

Select long twigs or slender branches stripped of leaves. Children may roll bits of cotton for pussy blooms. They may help tape these to the branches with Scotch tape. These are especially interesting to the children in the springtime.

BUNNY COTTON PICKER

Provide a round ice cream carton, a supply of cotton, long bristles from a brush, gray construction paper and paste.

Cut the carton to about 2 inches in height. Cut a hole the size of a nickel in the lid, near the edge. This is the back of the bunny. Fill carton with cotton. Make a pattern of the front of the bunny and trace on grey construction paper. Child may draw in face, color and cut out. Paste bristles on face for whiskers. Paste the bunny front on the end of carton without the hole. Pull cotton from hole in box to form tail. Now, when cotton is needed, pull out from tail and pinch off. This will make a delightful gift for the family or relatives.

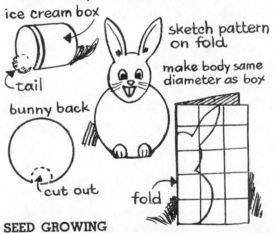

ice cream box

tail

bunny back

cut out

sketch pattern on fold

make body same diameter as box

fold

SEED GROWING

Use a flat box top and place a sheet of cotton in it. Place seeds such as beans or squash on cotton. Let children keep it moist and the seeds will sprout. The children will be delighted with this project. It will offer many opportunities to talk about God's wonderful world and the way He causes the seeds to grow.

DECALS (Decalcomania)
(*Also see* BOTTLES AND JARS *and* CANS.)

WALL PLAQUES, PAPER WEIGHTS

For these articles provide: tile squares (available at any tile supply store), decals of your choice, cloth suspension hangers, scraps of flannel or suede paper, paper towels.

Select decals and place in pan of water for a few seconds. Remove and place upside down in desired position on tiles. Remove paper and leave designs. Press excess water away with paper towel. Allow to dry. Place gummed hanger on back of tile for plaque. Add flannel or suede paper on back of tile for paper weight.

These crafts make excellent gifts for father and mother.

For Mother

For Father

paperwieght

SOAP GIFTS

Provide a bar of white toilet soap for each child, assorted decals, cellophane paper, Scotch tape or flower seals, paper towels.

Let children select the decal they wish to use. Place decals in water for a few seconds. Remove and place upside down on smooth side of soap. Remove paper from decal and leave design. Press excess water away with paper towel. After soap is dry, wrap in cellophane and seal with Scotch tape or gummed stickers. These make lovely gifts for any member of the family. They are especially nice if matched with other gifts decorated with decals.

BOTTLED GIFTS

BATH SALTS, WITCH HAZEL

Gather bottles of assorted sizes and as attractive as possible (lotion, sauce, liquid soap bottles, etc.), assorted decals, supply of bath salts, supply of witch hazel, ribbon or yarn, small plain card, greeting cards.

Apply decals to bottles, decorating tops if possible. For mother or big sister place bath salts in bottles, and for father add witch hazel for after shaving. Tie a bit of ribbon around neck of bottle. Help child write his name on a small card decorated with design from used greeting cards. Tie card on ribbon. Match these gifts with soap gifts if possible.

gift card

bath salts

witch hazel

OILCLOTH DOILIES

Provide oilcloth in any desired color (white or ivory preferred), decals, paper towels.

Cut oilcloth into squares, ovals, oblong or round designs with pinking shears before children arrive. Provide one doily for each child and let him apply decals where desired after soaking them in water. Absorb excess water with paper towels. If there are extra doilies, let children make them into matching sets for the Sunday school nursery.

OILCLOTH SCARF (or plastic)

For this project provide white or pastel colored oilcloth or plastic. Cut out with pinking shears to a length of 18, 24, or 30 inches, width in proportion. Provide an assortment of decals and paper towels.

Let the children apply the decals after soaking them in water for a few moments. Remove paper and absorb excess water with towels. For gift wrapping these may be rolled in wrapping paper. These will be welcome gifts for use in the kitchen, bathroom, service porch, summer cottage and the church nursery.

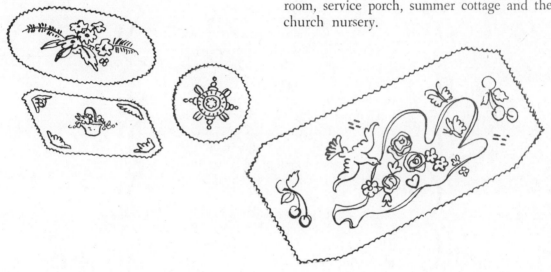

FINGER FUN
and
FINGER PAINTING

Little children are never still for a moment, unless they are sleeping! This is the way they grow. Finger fun and finger painting offer avenues of activity loved by these little folk around the world. Be alert to every opportunity to use these projects in ways that will help the Christian development of your preschoolers. Encourage each one to express himself when making the finger puppets or when painting. Use these activities following the telling of a Bible story or finger play and you will be able to have a glimpse of how a little child thinks about what he has heard. Win his confidence with sincere interest in his activity.

FINGER FUN

FINGER PUPPETS

Gather old white cotton gloves, scissors and colored pencils.

Help children draw faces on finger tips of clean white gloves. If they cannot color the faces, they can color the backs of the heads. Cut the ends of the glove fingers off about one to three-fourths inch from the tip. These will fit on the child's hands and he will have five "puppets"—one for each finger of his right hand. Use any favorite finger plays to tell "stories" or have activity fun. Or, the teacher can lead the children in "follow the leader" finger activity. If colored gloves are available, use red, yellow, black, white and brown for all the children of the world.*

* A book of finger plays, **Fascinating Finger Fun**, is available through the publisher of this book, or from your nearest religious book store.

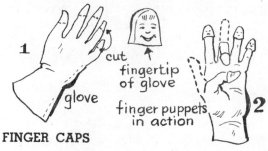

FINGER CAPS

Cut out pictures of children and adults to represent fathers and mothers. Provide five strips of white paper size 1 x ½ inches for each child, some paste and Scotch tape.

Let children cut the heads off the paper figures and paste in the center of the white strips. Help the children to make a finger family—a mother, father, brother, sister and little baby. When the heads are pasted on the slips, make finger caps by taping the paper to fit the children's fingers: father is for the thumb, mother for the index finger, etc. Use favorite finger plays with children as they wear the finger caps.

STOCKING PUPPET

Provide the following for each puppet: one stocking, cotton preferred, with top about 10 inches from heel; colored pencils, scissors, rubber band, 12-inch piece of ribbon or narrow piece of gingham, ball of cotton (enough to stuff head), string.

Tie stocking tightly between toe and heel on wrong side. Turn stocking. The back of the heel will form the face of the puppet and the toe will help pad the head. Put sufficient cotton in the heel to round out the head. Color back of head for hair and draw in a face with the colored pencils. Put a rubber band under the head, leaving sufficient room for index finger to be inserted into head. Tie colored ribbon or gay piece of gingham around neck and into a bow. Cut two holes in stocking, one on each side, for arms. Thumb and middle finger will form arms and index finger will fit into the head. Now the puppet is ready to act! This little figure can help tell many Bible stories and be used for finger fun activity.

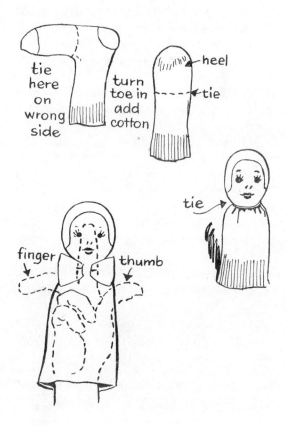

FINGER PAINTING

Finger painting is a favorite craft activity with small children. It is a fine therapeutic aid for handicapped children as well as a delightful medium for creative art. It is most successful when the children are divided into small groups. It may be done indoors, outdoors, at home, at Vacation Bible School, or wherever craft activities are supervised.

No brushes are necessary as the painting is done with fingers. Cover the table with linoleum, oilcloth, or any washable surface. Obtain regular finger-paint paper which is glazed on one side, or large sheets of newsprint. Finger paints may be obtained from any art or craft store, or you can make them. Wet the paper thoroughly in a flat pan or sink. Drain and smooth it, glazed surface up, on the table. Smooth out all air bubbles and wrinkles. Use wooden spatulas and put daubs of paint (about a teaspoonful) in center of the paper. Use one hand, spread out, and rub the paint over the entire surface of the paper. If paint should dry, add water. The designs will vary as upward strokes are used, wriggling lines, horizontal strokes. Both hands may be used, once the paper is covered with paint. Then other colors may be used over the basic covering. All work must be done while the paint is wet. When painting is finished, lift it by the corners and place it on cardboard or newspapers to dry. Do not leave it on the table. When dry, press on reverse side with hot iron to remove wrinkles.

There is great opportunity for the children to use their imagination in this activity. Ask them to tell you about what they are making. (Never ask the child, "What is it?") Suggest that they might paint something that will remind them of a favorite Bible story.

FINGER PAINT RECIPES

Two recipes are given below. Choose the one easiest and most economical for your group to have. Provide one jar for each color of paint and keep the jars covered when not in use. Each recipe should make about four scant pints and should take care of about twenty children.

> 1 quart of water
> 3 tablespoons of starch
> 1 tablespoon of flour
> A few drops of oil of wintergreen
> Calcimine powder for coloring.

Add a small amount of water to the starch and flour and make a smooth paste. Boil the rest of the water and add paste. Cook until thick, adding a few drops of oil of wintergreen to keep paint from forming scum. Add calcimine powder for coloring, mixing in small amounts until desired color is obtained. Cool and store in jars.

> 1½ cups laundry starch (about one box)
> 1 quart of water
> 1½ cups soap flakes
> ½ cup talcum (may be omitted)
> Poster paints or vegetable coloring
> (assorted colors)

Mix starch with a little cold water, sufficient to form paste. Boil quart of water and mix with paste, stirring constantly. Cook until mixture becomes transparent. Add talcum and let mixture cool a bit. Add soap flakes and stir until smooth. Cool and pour into jars. Add coloring and seal jars.

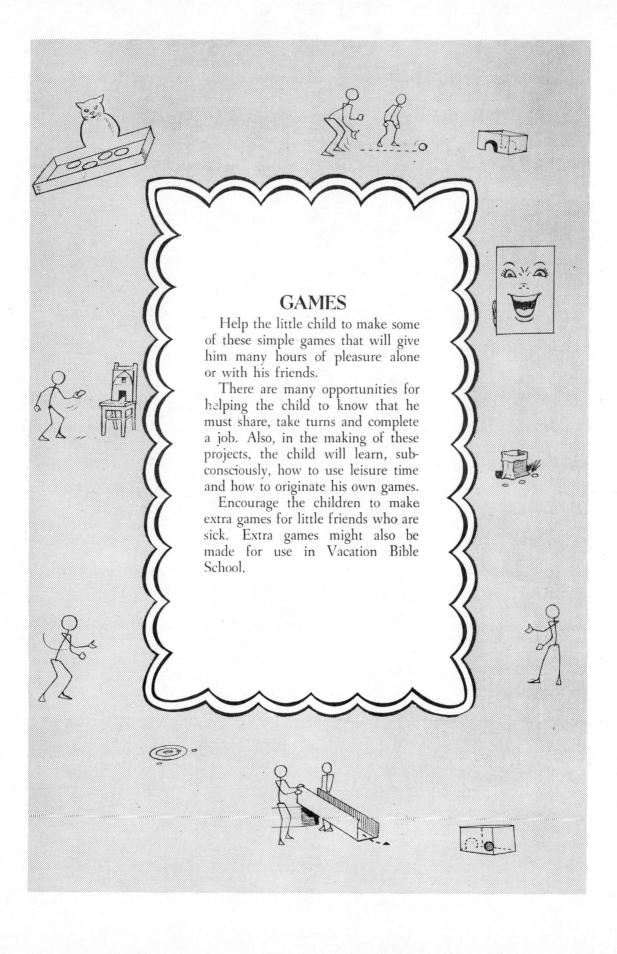

GAMES

Help the little child to make some of these simple games that will give him many hours of pleasure alone or with his friends.

There are many opportunities for helping the child to know that he must share, take turns and complete a job. Also, in the making of these projects, the child will learn, subconsciously, how to use leisure time and how to originate his own games.

Encourage the children to make extra games for little friends who are sick. Extra games might also be made for use in Vacation Bible School.

GAMES
(Also see TOYS, SPOOLS
and MAILING TUBES.)

WALK IN BOX

Gather odd-size boxes large enough for child to step into. Remove tops. Distribute boxes across room to form a path. Let children take turns walking, making sure they use boxes for the path. When a child misses a step in a box, he is out of the game.

TUNNEL BALL

Cut openings in opposite sides of a large cardboard carton. Object of the game is for the child to roll the ball through both openings. Teacher should keep track of the score to declare a winner.

FUN BAND

After children make a drum, rhythm band shaker (see *Toys*) a hummer (see *Mailing Tubes*) and other rhythm instruments, let them form a band and play a tune, preferably a march, such as "Onward Christian Soldiers."

BUTTONS AND BAGS

Provide children with white paper sacks and crayons. Let them color the sacks. Roll tops of sacks (bags) down two folds and stand up. Provide an assortment of buttons, giving each child six. Children may stand a few feet from bags and toss in buttons. The one who puts the most buttons in his bag wins.

BUTTON TARGET

Provide each child with a large plain paper plate and a red crayon. Color plate like a target and place on floor. Give four buttons to each child and let him stand a few feet from target and toss buttons. Object of the game is to place the buttons in the center.

RING THE NOSE

Each child will need a piece of cardboard about 15 x 20 inches, crayons, a large nail and 3 jar rubbers. Color face on cardboard and insert nail from back for nose. Place board on chair. Child stands a few feet in front of board and uses the rubber rings to toss over the nail nose.

BOUNCE THE BALLS FOR KITTY

Provide 4 milk bottle tops, crayons and a shoe box for each child. Let child color milk bottle tops red on one side and blue on the other side. Cut the box down for the child, leaving the kitten on one side as shown in sketch. Child may color bottom of the box and the kitten. Place the milk bottle tops (balls) in the box, blue side up. Object of the game is to bounce the tops until all four are red.

TUNNEL ROLL BALL

3 large corrugated boxes are needed for this game. One box will be used for a prop. Cut away flaps on another box and cut a tunnel opening in one side. The third box should be a long one with top and ends removed to form a ramp. Prop the long box on the "prop" carton with other end on the floor. Place tunnel box about two feet from end of long box. Object of the game is to roll the ball down the ramp into the tunnel. Several children may work together on this project, then take turns playing.

PIG IN THE BARN

Use the pattern for the bean bag pig. Have several "pigs" made up and on hand. Let children make a barn from a large piece of cardboard (the side of a corrugated cardboard carton will do). Cut out door for the pig and prop the barn on a chair. Object of the game is to put the pig through the barn door.

Pig Pattern—

Cut two pieces of plain cloth from this pattern. Be sure wrong sides of material face each other in cutting! Blanket stitch together, leaving small opening. Fill with dried beans and sew closed. Make a small loop for a tail.

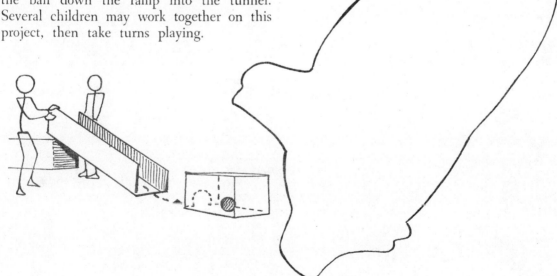

GARDENS AND PLANTERS

Gardens and planters add interest and attraction to the Sunday school and home. They also express thoughtfulness when used as gifts. The gardens and planters suggested here may be made by the children for their homes, school and for gifts. While making these gardens, the child may learn and recall stories of the creation, of God's gifts to us, and ways He helps things to grow. Never miss a teaching opportunity!

GARDENS AND PLANTERS

DISH GARDENS

1) BEET AND CARROT CREATION

Provide a round or square dish or pan, some pretty rocks, one carrot and one beet. Fill receptacle ⅔ full of water. Cut off all but one inch of the beet and carrot tops (cut off lower half of the vegetable too). Arrange carrot and beet with rocks in water. Place in the sun. The top part of the vegetables will grow and form lovely foliage. Small figurines may be placed in the garden.

2) TURNIP AND SWEET POTATO ARRANGEMENT

Select a medium-size sweet potato and cut in half. Prepare turnip in the same manner as the beet and carrot in previous arrangement. Place vegetables in a dish or pan so they will protrude above the water. Rocks and figurines may be added. Some water will be absorbed by the plants as they grow so keep the receptacle about ⅔ full of water.

DRY MARINE GARDEN

Gather together any pretty seashells, pebbles, colored rocks or coral you may have about the house. Put several handfuls of sand through a strainer to refine. Use a goldfish bowl, glass box, bowl, a large-base juice decanter or jar for the garden. Place sand in bottom and arrange sea shells, rocks, etc. Dried seaweed and tiny star fish may be added if you live in a seaboard area.

MARINE GARDEN IN WATER

Gather together the same items named in previous garden. After arrangement is complete, add enough water to cover sand but not enough to cover rocks. Purchase small turtles from a pet shop so each child may have one or two in his garden. Sometimes names are painted on the turtles' backs without charge. This will add interest. Explain how the turtles must be cared for. We are God's helpers to care for His creatures.

DESERT GARDEN

The children may be taken on an expedition to find pretty twigs, weeds, dried seed pods, rocks, etc., to make their gardens. Talk about God's wonderful world as you hunt for these things. Use a glass bowl, large-base jar or flat dish for each garden. Strain some sand. Twigs, seed pods, rocks, etc., may be arranged in interesting ways to make a desert garden. Little spool bunnies may be made and placed in the gardens. (See *Spools*.)

CITRUS PLANTER

Cut a milk carton in two, about 3 inches from the bottom. In this bottom part place a few rocks then some sandy soil. Save the seeds of grapefruit and place several in the planter. Keep seeds moist. Place wax container in a can or box, decorated with foil, raffia (see *Raffia Craft*) or pretty paper. Keep planter in the sun.

NASTURTIUM BOX

Cut an egg carton in half and place a small paper nut cup in each partition. Fill cups with soil and poke a nasturtium seed in each one. Keep soil moist and plants will mature and bloom. Child may paint egg carton planter with poster paints or color with crayons.

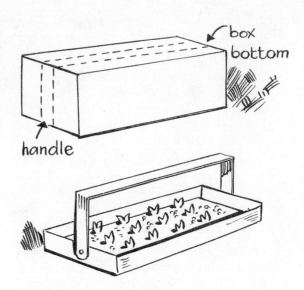

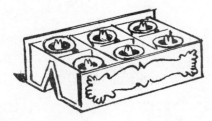

WINDOW BOX

Small wooden boxes are available at grocery stores for the asking. These make lovely window boxes. Fill the bottom of a box with small rocks and then add sand and soil. Plant growing sweet potato vines, carrot seed for foliage, nasturtiums, bulbs or pansies.

ARTIFICIAL FLOWER BOX

Select an attractive gift box or a shoe box, a dozen wooden spoons, scraps of assorted colors of paper, paste and pictures of flowers from seed catalogs or magazines.

Fold 2-inch diameter circles of colored paper and cut daisy patterns. Paste on spoons and paste yellow or brown dots in centers. Plain colored circles of paper may be used for poppies. Or, flowers from seed catalogs may be pasted on spoons. Add leaves to the handle "stems." Place flowers in the box filled with sand. (Also see *Boxes*, Flower Bed.)

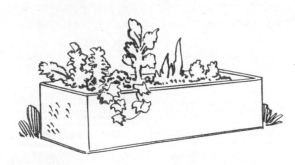

SEED BED

Use the top of a shoe box, envelope box or top of any sturdy box. Line with foil paper (kitchen variety). Cut a handle for seed bed from the bottom of the box, about 1½ inches wide. Cut handle lengthwise of box and the sides will form a natural handle without folding. Attach to seed bed with brads. Fill box with sandy soil and plant flowers or vegetable seeds which develop rapidly. Flowers that are best for each section of the country may vary. Check with your local nursery. Keep seed bed damp and in the sun. Use the project to speak often of God's plan for providing food and beautiful flowers.

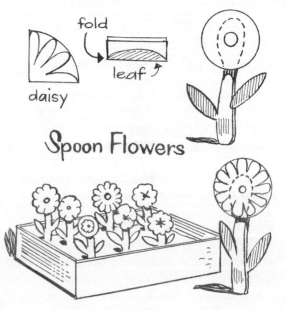

Spoon Flowers

GARMENT BAGS
GREETING CARDS
HANGERS

A little ingenuity and the above items can offer many happy and profitable hours for little people. Save these articles so you will have sufficient on hand for a group of children. Boys as well as girls will like to make dress-up clothes and wear them. Let them choose to be some Bible character. They might even design their own garments.

Use of the greeting cards and hangers will help the child to think of others as they make gifts and bird stations. Discuss the projects with the children and encourage them to think about the Bible truths learned through Bible stories.

GARMENT BAGS
(PAPER)

BOLERO SUIT

Cut garment bag as shown in the sketch. Child may color before cutting and after you have marked design with crayon. Fold bottom part of bag over as noted. Tie a string around the child's waist to hold skirt on child.

DRESS

Cut bag to desired length and let child design his garment and cut fringe at bottom. Cut clit down front for neck and fold back for collar. Use string or colored crepe paper for sash.

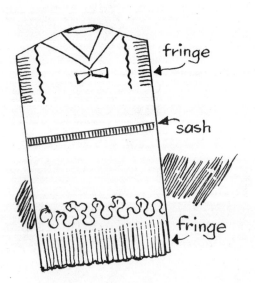

COAT

Cut bag to proper length for child. Let him color. Cut bag down the center and make slits in sides for belt. Use colored crepe paper for belt and insert through the slits so as to tie in front.

APRON AND PINAFORE

Cut garment bag as shown in the sketch to make an apron or pinafore. Let child color as he wishes after you have marked cutting lines but before you do any cutting. You may have to take a tuck in the side strips with a staple machine or safety pin. The apron may be worn while the child does finger painting, plaster work, etc. If pinafore style is desired for girls, crepe paper ruffles may be added across the shoulder.

SLEEPING BAG (Nap Sack)

Encourage children to rest at Vacation Bible School, in the Kindergarten, or in the home by crawling into this cozy sleeping bag that can be made from a garment bag. Let children color the bags, then line with several thicknesses of newspapers which you have stitched together ahead of time. Child may paste a picture on the outside of his bag for identification or print his name on the bag (with your help, of course). As soon as bags are completed let the children have a little rest period. Pull the shades and play a favorite hymn softly.

GREETING CARDS

Save all types of greeting cards: birthday, Christmas, get-well, congratulations, etc., and encourage your friends to save these kinds of cards for you. You will find many uses for them and will devise additional ways to make attractive crafts than those suggested here.

PIN AND NEEDLE HOLDERS

Paste or staple a piece of flannel or felt inside used Christmas or other greeting cards. Add a few pins and needles to the flannel. Missionaries will welcome these to use as gifts to the natives.

flannel

MIRRORS

Scour the neighborhood and home for pocket mirrors, particularly the double kind. Soak them briefly in water then pry apart. Paste Bible pictures from Christmas cards on the back of each piece of mirror. These are coveted awards among children and on mission fields.

back side of mirror

CALENDARS

Cut out flowers and other designs from greeting cards. Paste on light-weight cardboard about 5 x 7 inches. Obtain small calendar pads for children to paste on calendars. If calendar pads are not available, mimeograph monthly calendar sheets to paste on bottom of cardboard.

Monthly Calendar

Year Calendar

DON'T FORGET THE MISSIONARIES

Gather and save greeting cards. Cut away the personal notes, package and send to the missionaries. Be sure to check with the post office as to size and weight of package permissible to each mission field. Check with your missionaries as to duty regulations.

HANGERS
(WIRE)

NEST SUPPLY DEPOT FOR BIRDS

You will need a wire coat hanger, scraps of string and yarn, a mailing tube and some Scotch tape for this depot. Cut about 4 holes in each side of the tube, opposite each other, and slit the tube lengthwise between holes. Slip tube over bottom part of hanger and fasten together with Scotch tape. Children may put string and yarn through holes and let it hang down. Tie hanger in tree and watch birds gather string for their nests.

BIRD HOUSE

For this project you will need a wire coat hanger, a shoe box, the bottom or top of a box about 2 inches deep, a stapler, scissors and glue.

Bend hanger as shown in sketch 1. Cut hole in center of one end of bottom of shoe box. Cut window holes in center of box sides, near one end. Let child insert top of bent hanger in hole in end of box and hanger sides in window holes. (2) Cut door in one end of box top, being careful not to cut apart from the top at bottom of door. Let child fold this door hinge back to edge of box top, then glue fast or staple. (3) Cut corner of 2-inch box as shown in sketch and let child paste it above the door for a porch. (4) Glue lid on box with door at bottom of bird house. Now the bird house is ready to hang up. The hanger inside the box forms the perch for the bird.

Teacher and parent must help the child with this project which offers many opportunities to review the stories of God's care of us, His care of the birds, His creation of the birds, etc.

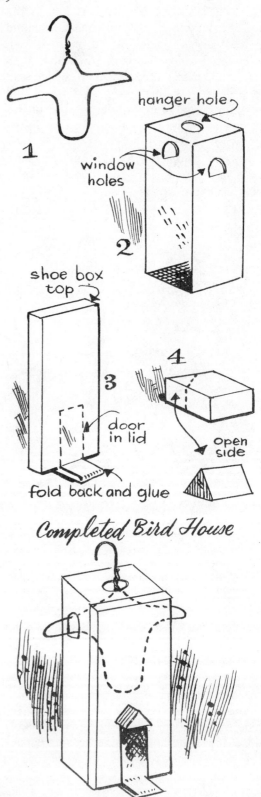

MAILING TUBES

As you make up samples of these items, think of the ways you can direct the conversation later on when you work with the children. They will need more help on these projects than on some because of the cutting, so arrange to have some of the tubes cut in advance of the time needed. Many of these items would make acceptable gifts to children in hospitals or orphanages.

MAILING TUBES
(Also see *Christmas, Games, Toys*.)

Save all varieties of mailing tubes: from wax paper, paper towels, shelf paper, calendars, dress materials, etc. Consult your drug store, variety store and dry goods store for tubes. Encourage the children to think of others as well as themselves while making craft projects.

NAPKIN RINGS

Provide a tube about 1½ inches in diameter, crayons (also paint or colored pencils), and cellophane tape.

Cut rings from tube about 1 inch wide. Color with crayons. Or, child can make a design by wrapping ring with cellophane tape. Assist child in writing his name, or names of his family, and trace on rings. Extras may be made for guests.

BRACELETS

For these articles provide colored cellophane tape, colored pencils or crayolas, paste, glitter in assorted colors and tubes cut in ½ inch widths.

Cut bracelets for child and let him color or decorate with cellophane tape. Or, he may cover outside with paste and sprinkle on glitter. For easy use of glitter, put it in salt shakers and place articles on paper. After using the glitter pour the excess from paper back into container.

BINOCULARS

Provide two tubes about 1¼ inches in diameter and 6 inches long, brown or black crayons, butcher tape about 2 inches wide, piece of string about 25 inches long.

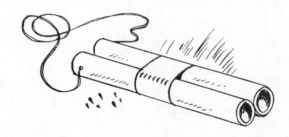

Bind two tubes together with butcher tape and color. Punch holes, one in each tube on opposite sides, and fasten string for carrying binoculars around neck.

AFRICAN HOUSES

For each house provide a drinking cup, cornucopia style; tube the same diameter as the cups, excelsior, paste and scissors.

Cut the tube in 3¼ inch lengths. Color brown. Cut or draw in a door. Cover cup with paste and sprinkle on excelsior until covered.

When cup is dry place on tube "house" for roof. Cover a large piece of cardboard with paste and sprinkle on some strained sand. Stand several houses on cardboard to form a village. Use this background for telling a missionary story.

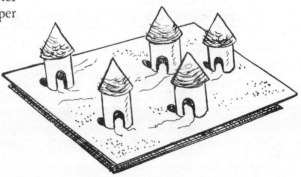

RING TOSS GAME

Provide the following for each game: a tube about 12 inches long and 1½ inches in diameter, a tube about 3 inches in diameter (a salt box or round cereal box will do nicely), piece of heavy cardboard (corrugated box is fine) about 14 inches square, a piece of cardboard about 10 inches square, butcher tape, colored cellophane tape and glue.

Color long tube a bright color or wrap with colored cellophane, barber pole style. Cut one end of tube into eighths, 1½ inches from end. Bind large piece of cardboard with butcher tape and cut hole in center the same diameter as the tube. Insert tube into hole so that cut end may be spread on underside of cardboard. Fasten securely with glue. Paste 10-inch square of cardboard over glued surface to assure sturdiness. Now cut rings from the large tube, about ¾ inch wide, 3 for each child. Let each child color his rings and the game is ready. The winner is the one who tosses the most rings over the post.

spread tube

back side

butcher tape binding

toss ring

ROLL GAME

For this game you will need a tube 12 inches long and 1½ inches in diameter, some colored paper or wallpaper to cover tube, a corrugated carton about 24 inches long.

Cut the tube into four 3-inch lengths. Cover these with wallpaper or color. Cut three openings 4 inches wide in the corrugated box after flaps have been removed. Object of game is to roll the cylinders into the holes.

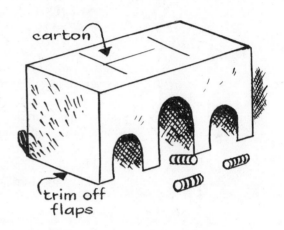

carton

trim off flaps

HUMMER

Provide a tube 12 inches long and 1 inch in diameter, a rubber band, a large nail, wax paper (4-inch square) or two thicknesses of tissue paper, wallpaper, crayolas or paints.

Cover tube with wallpaper or color. Punch 5 to 8 holes in one end of tube with nail. On same end fasten wax paper with rubber band. Hum into opposite end. Let children use these to accompany the rhythm band. They might make extra ones for children who are convalescing.

rubber band

holes

EXTRA SUGGESTIONS FOR CRAFT FUN
(Miscellaneous)

Every teacher will want to reserve a place for miscellaneous ideas. Tucked in this section of the book are just a few for starters. Paste other ideas in the back of the book and place still more in a craft file or box where they will be *used*.

The ideas here are to prime your own ingenuity and originality. Everyone has an innate desire for self-expression — teacher and child. Use these ideas for that stimulus. Look about and consider how native materials can be used, jot down ideas, share your enthusiasm, try your initiative. You will be pleasantly amazed and the children will reward your expectation with accomplishment.

MISCELLANEOUS

ENVELOPE TELEVISION

Any size envelope may be used for this project although the large size of 4½ x 9½ inches is preferred. Cut a window in address side, snip ends, and seal envelope. Child may color both sides. Cut a strip of paper about 30 inches long and four inches wide then cut out pictures of animals, people, or Bible pictures, etc. and paste on strip. When strip is full of pictures, slip through cut ends of the envelope and paste together. The pictures may be pulled through the envelope and viewed. The children might make one of these to correlate with a quarter's Sunday school lessons they are studying.

MILK BOTTLE CAP BELT

Gather round milk bottle caps and let child color the plain side. Punch two holes on opposite sides and help child string on two shoestrings as shown in sketch. Make the belt to fit child then tie shoestrings together and let ends hang. The ends can be made into a bow tie when child wears belt.

A CHEW-ME GIFT

A package of gum, a crayon and a folded piece of construction paper are needed for this clever gift. The child may draw two circles, one for a head and one for a body. Paste two sticks of gum for arms and two for legs. Draw a face on Gum-Boy and he is ready to send to a little sick friend. The maker may chew the fifth piece of gum.

SCRAPBOOKS

Use discarded (clean) window blinds and stitch into scrapbooks. (Generous pieces of blind fabrics may be had for the asking at variety stores where blinds are cut to order.) Various sizes of books may be made, according to width of material available. Children may paste in pictures of children, Bible scenes, nature pictures, etc. These scrapbooks are welcome in hospitals, Sunday school, Vacation Bible School, the nursery, or in the home. The making of these offers an opportunity to teach thoughtfulness and to encourage initiative.

KITTEN MATCH SCRATCHER

Materials needed: one piece of colored construction paper, an oval piece of sandpaper, two pieces of colored yarn, paste, crayon, Scotch tape.

Paste the oval piece of sandpaper in the center of the construction paper, slipping the yarn (about 3-inch piece) just under the lower end of the sandpaper. Draw a cat's head above the sandpaper body. Use another piece of yarn and make a loop on the back of the construction paper, fastening it with Scotch tape for a hanger. If you wish, have the children make the cat's head out of colored construction paper to match the yarn tail.

SOAP BOATS

Use a medium-size bar of Ivory soap and cut in two. Or, use small guest sizes of Ivory soap. Obtain medical sticks and place in the center of the soap bar for a mast. Prepare paper sails for the children to slip over these masts. The boats will sail when placed in water.

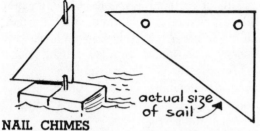

actual size of sail →

NAIL CHIMES

Six nails (one extra long one), some linen thread, and a 12-inch stick or ruler will make these chimes. Tie all except the longest one about 2 inches apart on the stick. One child may hold the stick by the ends while another strikes the nails, one at a time, with the longest nail. The results are a chime-like ring. Children may take turns striking the nails.

These chime sets are excellent to use with a rhythm band, with children in the Nursery Department, or with quiet singing.

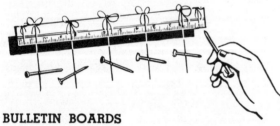

BULLETIN BOARDS

Provide a piece of 18-inch square double corrugated cardboard and some Trimz border wallpaper. Help the child wet the wallpaper strip, which comes gummed, and paste around the edge of the cardboard. A delightful Noah's Ark design is available in this type of border. Punch two holes in the cardboard and attach a light-weight rope for a hanger. Now the child has his own bulletin board where he may post his Sunday school paper, pictures, handcraft projects, etc.

Make a larger one of these for the Sunday school room and for the child's play room.

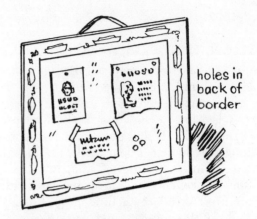

holes in back of border

BOOK AND BOX COVERS

These are accepted gifts by mother and father, older brother or sister. After the child makes marble paper (see *Recipes*, Marble Paper), and when it is dry, help him cover a book or box.

PINE CONE POODLE

Provide 1 pine cone, 2 gummed reinforcements and a 4-inch length of chenille wire.

Paste gummed reinforcements at broad end of pine cone to make face. Twist wire around pine cone about ⅓ of way from "face" to make front legs. Now he's your poodle doggie!

gummed re-inforce-ments

chenille wire

METAL NAPKIN HOLDER

Salvage one roll cover from some adhesive tape. Cover with colored Scotch tape. Large and small rolls make suitable rings for napkins.

FREE-HAND PAINTING

Let the children choose the subjects which they wish to paint, suggested perhaps by Sunday school lessons, Bible stories, etc. The calcimine paint (see *Finger Painting*) which is easy to make, may be diluted and placed in empty baby food cans. Place cans in wood or metal glass holders to prevent spilling. Ordinary long-handle house-paint brushes up to 1½ inches wide are suitable. If you do not have low easels, children may clip the newsprint or drawing paper to a heavy piece of cardboard with clothspins. Prop cardboard on chairs after covering them with newspapers. Ask children to tell you the story they have painted.

PEN WIPER AND BLOTTER

Materials needed: colored blotter paper about 5 inches square (four pieces), one brad, gummed reinforcements, scissors, pencil, pattern of butterfly, flower, animal, etc.

Provide a number of designs and cut out on cardboard. These are simple to make by enlarging pattern on graph paper after you have found a picture of what you wish to use. Children like flowers, animals, butterflies, etc. Keep design simple. Trace cardboard design on each of the four colors of blotter paper and cut out. Punch hole in center and insert brad. Decorate with gummed reinforcements. Colored flannel or felt may be substituted for blotter paper.

Enlarge butterfly on graph paper to scale of 1 in. squares

brad

RELISH SUSAN

For this project each child will need ½ of a small rubber ball, 1 chocolate candy cup, 2 crayons, colored toothpicks, paste, and a paper plate (medium size, about 4-inch diameter).

Child may color paper plate and paste candy cup in bottom, flattened out. Color half rubber ball and paste to center of candy paper. This forms the toothpick or relish holder. Toothpicks may be inserted into ball. Mother will be glad to have such a lovely gift as this Relish Susan to hold pickles, olives, etc.

toothpicks

DAISY PINCUSHION

Provide the following for each child: ½ of a small rubber ball, a 4-inch square of yellow construction paper, a 5-inch square of orange construction paper, a 7-inch square of green contruction paper, glue, scissors and a gummed hanger.

Fold colored squares of construction paper 4 times and cut petals. Glue yellow petals to orange ones and orange petals to green ones. Paste half ball to the center of the yellow paper for pincushion. Add gummed hanger to back of green paper for hanging. Or, the pincushion can be used when it is placed flat on a shelf or bureau.

fold

green

ball

Yellow

orange

TOUCH-AND-FEEL FUN

Little children "see" with their hands as well as with their eyes. It is fun to "see" pictures that have been animated and it is fun to make them so.

Keep a box of "touch and feel" items handy. These include bits of cloth, ribbon, ruffling, cellophane tape, sandpaper, cotton, string, blotter paper, tiny buttons, flocking, feathers, satin, excelsior, berry boxes, and odds and ends of all kinds which might lend an interesting "feel" to pictured objects.

Paste or tape these items to magazine pictures, story book pictures, Sunday school papers, or reproductions of pictures. For instance, feathers may be pasted on birds, cotton on sheep, broom straws on a basket, leather scrap on a Bible or shoes, berry box scraps on houses or buildings, satin or gingham on clothing. It is not necessary to cover the entire object, but just paste or tape enough of the materials to make the picture attractive to the touch as well as the eye.

Encourage the children to make scrapbooks of touch-and-feel pictures for other boys and girls. This type of work is not only an encouragement to ingenuity, but stimulates the child to think of others because he wants to share that which intrigues him.

PAPER

Newpapers   **Paper Doilies**
Paper Bags   **Paper Plates**
Paper Cups   **Paper Straws**
Paper Cutting and Folding

Gather the above paper articles and just see how much fun the children will have making hats, dresses, faces, clowns, trees, flowers, dolls, place mats, fans, masks, pictures and toys.

The use of these household articles will spark, in the minds of the children, the desire to create new objects. Be alert to guide this desire into profitable activities and a motivation to make something for others. Never discourage a child, but spur him on to further effort and accomplishment. Do not expect him to comply with adult standards, for he always produces at his own level of ability.

NEWSPAPERS

A DORCAS COAT

Every child may wear a little coat to remind him of kind Dorcas in the Bible who made clothing for many friends and little children. Use a double fold of newspaper and fold over once again. Help child cut a neck hole. Unfold. Cut down front. Child may color coat, then put on.

If several children make a coat, let them put their coats on and then be seated on the floor. Tell the story of Dorcas.

INDIAN HEADDRESS

Use a double sheet of newspaper, unfolded. Double lengthwise and help child cut "feathers" about 1½ inch wide to within 2 inches of the fold. Fasten about head with Scotch tape and let remainder of "feathers" hang down back. The children might play a little game or be seated, after a march around the room, and hear a missionary story.

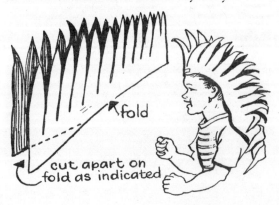

SOLDIER HATS

Use a one-page sheet from any newspaper. Two styles of hats can be made: (1) one by stopping after step 3 and (2) the other by completing all seven steps. Use the No. 1 plan for small children and tape the sides of the hat together. Practice folding the No. 2 hat so the older children can follow the instructions without difficulty.

(1) Fold newspaper in half. (2) Fold corners down to center leaving x - x extending. (3) Fold x - x up on opposite sides. (Tape these sides together for an easy-to-make hat). (4) Slip thumbs into No. 3, spread and fold into a square, tucking one flap under the other. (5) Fold on a - b, bringing points up on opposite sides. (6) Slip thumbs into peak inside, spread and fold in form square illustrated in step 6. (7) Catch points at top between thumb and fingers and shape into hat.

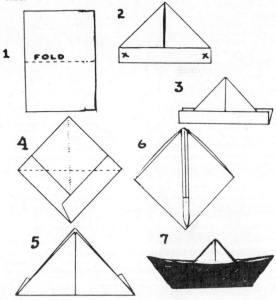

PAPER BAGS

Little children can have bags of fun with paper sacks. Provide paper bags (14-pound size), paste, crayons, feathers, broom straws, black yarn or crepe paper, newspapers, string, clothespins, feathers, gold stars. From these supplies the children can make paper faces, a horse, some hats and a crown.

PAPER FACES

Place bags over children's heads. Mark places for eyes. Cut out eyes, if desired, so children can see through them. Let children choose faces they wish to make. Suggestions for some are given. Shorten bags if necessary.

DONKEY

Draw eyes and nose on bag. Cut two pieces of paper 1½ x 4 inches from another sack and paste on sides of bag, at top, for ears. Cut one piece of paper 1½ x 3 inches and color red. Paste on bag for tongue.

PUSSY

Draw eyes, nose and mouth on paper bag. Cut two strips of paper 2½ x 2 inches and taper at one end. These will make the ears. Paste them on the sides of the bag. Select several broom straws and Scotch tape them on face for whiskers.

CLOWN

Draw face on bag to resemble clown and color. Let child cut a circle 5 inches in diameter (or provide one for him) from another paper bag. Cut this in half and paste on sides of bag for ears. Cut a large circle from a newspaper (a double fold, folded once) and cut in fourths. One fourth will form a cone for a hat which may be pasted or pinned to the bag. Cut a tassel from colored crepe paper and paste on end of hat.

man with glasses

MAN WITH GLASSES

Draw hair, face and glasses on sack with crayons.

CHINAMAN

Provide black yarn or crepe paper for children to braid for a queue. Make it about 12 inches long and paste in middle of top of bag. Fasten a strip of black paper, several inches long to mouth for a mustache. Make ears by cutting a 4-inch circle in half and pasting on sides of bag. Draw face and hair on bag with crayons.

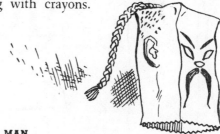

OLD MAN

Draw face, hair and ears on bag. Cut away sides and back then cut strips in front piece to form beard.

HORSE

Choose a large bag for a horse's head. Cut two pieces of paper 1¼ x 4 inches from another bag and paste on sides of first bag for ears. Stuff newspapers into sack and tie it on a broom stick for the head. Child may also cut newspaper strips for a mane and tail. Fasten mane to head and stick. Tack tail about 15 inches from opposite end of stick. Use rope or heavy string for reins.

For variation, clothespins may be used for ears and a small bell may be placed around the horse's neck.

HATS

BASEBALL HAT

Use a merchandise bag, one with the envelope style bottom. Choose one 9 inches wide if possible. Tuck in corners of bag. Cut away back of bag and cut a visor in front. Color. (See sketch.)

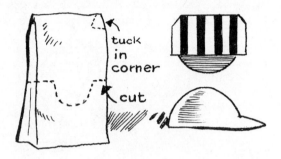

SOLDIER'S HAT

Tuck in corners of bag as for baseball hat. Cut off bag 6 inches from seam end. Fold bottom up 2 inches to make band. Paste gummed stars on band. Children may wear these after they are made and march about singing "Onward Christian Soldiers."

ROBINHOOD HAT

Tuck in corners of an 8 or 9-inch bag. Cut off bag 4 inches from seam end. Insert a feather on one side near one end. This will be the front of the hat. If feathers are not available, teachers may cut some from cardboard. Children may color the feathers red and the hat green.

MESSENGER HAT

Use a 10 or 12-pound grocery bag. Cut it off 6 inches from the bottom and fold up 2 inches. Color. Let children wear these to perform errands.

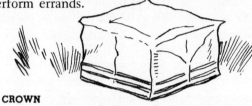

CROWN

Select a paper bag to fit the child's head and cut off end, leaving about a 6-inch band. Child may color crown and paste on gold stars.

PAPER CUPS

There are many uses for paper cups in craft work. Children will enjoy seeing how many projects can be worked out and they will be able to suggest others after you have introduced one or more of those presented here. Be sure to make up samples of all the crafts you plan for the children to make. Encourage their attempts to create new ideas.

WIGWAM

Use a cornucopia style paper cup. Cut an angular slit and fold flap back for door. Use two colored toothpicks and stick in top for poles. Children may color as desired.

Talk about the Indian peoples and the work our missionaries do among them. Children may make an Indian village.

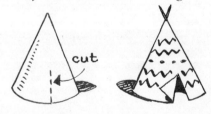

AFRICAN HUT

Provide two paper cups, one a straight style with a flat bottom and one cornucopia style. Also have some paste, cardboard and bit of excelsior handy. Color straight cup brown and draw in a door. Cover other cup with film of paste and sprinkle on bits of straw. Place straw covered cup on top of straight cup. Place these huts on a piece of cardboard.

Talk about the children who live in houses like these and how we can help them hear about Jesus. Tell a missionary story and show pictures if possible.

BASKETS

Gather assorted plain paper cups, a bit of colored crepe paper, gummed seals, cardboard for handles, ½-inch brads. Decorate cups with gummed stickers. Make a ruffle of crepe paper and glue to edge of cup. Cut cardboard handle strips ½ inch wide and fasten with brads. Baskets can also be made by pasting on gummed stars or by covering with glitter or flocking.

PARTY HATS

Provide several 2-inch strands of yarn or narrow strips of crepe paper and a cornucopia paper cup. Cut tip off cup and insert yarn or crepe paper for tassels. Add a dab of paste inside the cup to hold tassel. Punch holes on each side of drinking end of cup and tie colored yarn for under-chin ties.

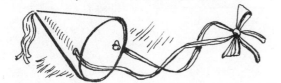

TREES

Provide a sucker stick, some clay and a cornucopia drinking cup for each tree. Child may color cup green, or cover it with a thin coat of paste and sprinkle on a bit of green flocking. Place sucker stick in ball of clay and put cup upside down on stick.

Use these trees with the Indian wigwams or African huts in creating villages.

clay

BELLS

Gather assorted sizes of paper cups, some round beads, flat buttons about the size of a nickel, colored yarn or ribbon, gummed stars, gummed flower seals or flowers cut from greeting cards.

Decorate cups as desired with stickers, crayons, etc. String a bead or button in center of a length of yarn or ribbon for a clapper. Measure length of clapper by depth of cup and tie a knot. Select a large flat button and string above knot. Punch hole in bottom of cup with a pencil and run ribbon ends through hole and tie in a bow.

FOLDED BOAT

Help the child fold a boat as described in section on *Newspapers*. Color. Melt some paraffin and let the child dip the bottom of the boat in paraffin. When the wax is dry the boat will float. The children might make several, different sizes.

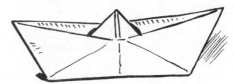

PAPER CUTTING AND FOLDING

PAPER DOLLS

Fold a sheet of paper in half then fold twice, lengthwise. Cut free-hand or trace a pattern of a doll for the child and help him to cut carefully on the lines. Draw faces on dolls or cut faces from magazines and paste on. The dolls can be pasted on a piece of construction paper. Write the words, "Jesus loves me," on the dolls for each child, one word to a doll. Or, color dolls the color of the races: red, yellow, black, brown. One can be left white.

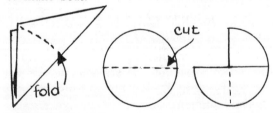

CIRCLE BOATS

Fold a square piece of paper in half twice. Then fold in half diagonally. Draw a line from center points to one-fourth distance from top point. Cut on line. Unfold and cut circle in half. Paste halves at right angles to make boat.

PENNANT BOAT

Fold a piece of oblong paper in the center, lengthwise. Make a diagonal cut from fold corner to opposite corner. Unfold and cut one-fourth of triangle off from wide end.

Turn this piece upside down and paste on colored construction paper to form hull of ship. Paste remaining piece onto hull for sail.

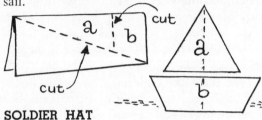

SOLDIER HAT

The size of hat is determined by the width of paper and the width should be about one-half of the circumference of the child's head. The length should be two and one-half times as long as the width.

Fold paper in half, widthwise, then fold corners down to center. Fold the two ends up on opposite sides. Tape ends to hold hat secure for wearing. Child may color hat and paste gummed stars on band. Help him write his name on band. Child may wear hat and join others in singing, "Onward Christian Soldiers."

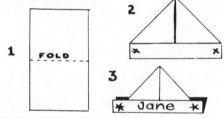

EASTER CROSS

After folding a boat as suggested above, make two cuts with scissors from bottom of boat as shown in sketch. (Omit dipping boat in paraffin.) Unfold. Cut off one fold at top. See the cross?

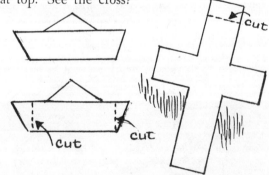

PARTY BONNET

Use a paper sack 5 or 6 inches wide. Cut off 4 inches from bottom. Cut up 1 inch at all four corners and fold. Cut off one folded strip. Cut two round doilies in half. Paste one half of these doilies on each side, fold-up; place the two half sections on the front of the bonnet and fold up. Attach strings to each side of sack.

(White sacks make the nicest bonnets if they are available.)

PAPER PLATES

CLOCK

Provide 9-inch paper plates. Cut out number squares from calendars. Make clock hands from a ½ inch strip of cardboard. Cut the large hand 3½ inches long and the smaller hand 2½ inches long. Help children paste numbers on back of paper plate and fasten hands on clock with a ½ inch paper brad. Fasten bit of yarn at top of "clock" for hanging.

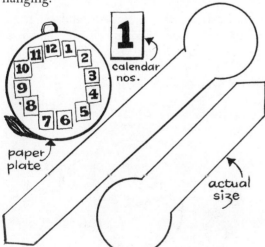

CALENDAR

Provide one 4-inch and one 9-inch paper plate for each child.

Also provide paste, small calendars, colored ribbon, crayons, sacred pictures from cards or calendars.

Let children select a picture of the nativity or some other religious subject. Paste it in the center of the large paper plate. Color edges of plates. Paste small calendar in center of small plate. Fasten plates together with small length of ribbon. Use a bit of ribbon for a wall hanger.

FAN

Use two fluted-edge plates 9 inches in diameter and a thin 10-inch length of wood about ¼ inch wide. Color plates or paste pictures on them. Paste plates together, back to back, with stick between them. Thumbtacks may also be used to keep the stick from slipping out.

CANDY TRAY

Provide one paper plate, one doily, one 12-inch strip of cardboard ½ inch wide, two ½-inch brads, crayons and paste.

Color doilies then paste on paper plate. Color edge of plate and cardboard strip which will be used as the handle. Fasten handle to opposite sides of plate with brads.

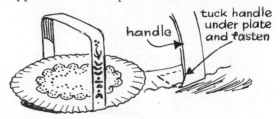

HAT

Use fluted edge plates, paper doilies, ribbon, paste and pictures of flowers. Turn plate upside down. Color doily or paste pictures of flowers on them. Paste completed doily on bottom of plate. Fasten a ribbon tie on each side of plate for hat.

MASKS

Use fluted 9-inch paper plates, 2-inch strips of crepe paper (black, brown, yellow, red), string, crayons, scissors.

Cut out eye holes for child. Color face. Show child how to ruffle crepe paper. Paste ruffle around face for hair. Let child choose color of "hair." Fasten string in sides of plate and tie mask around face.

crepe paper hair

"THANK YOU" PLATES

Provide each child with one plate, crayons, paste, ribbon or yarn, and a little table grace (mimeographed or typed).

Let children draw food on plate. Talk about how God provides our food. Give each child a copy of the table grace to paste on the plate after it is colored. Attach ribbon hanger for hanging plate on wall.

If this project is used with little children during Vacation Bible School, give the children some cookies and milk and let them repeat the prayer before they eat.

POTTED PLANT

Provide 6 or 7-inch paper plates, narrow thin sticks, thumbtacks, milk cartons, sand. Draw flower designs on plates. Tack flowers to sticks. Cut milk carton in half and fill bottom part with sand. Place flower in the sand.

Flowers can also be made by pasting small plates inside the larger plates after they are colored.

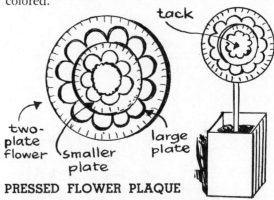

tack

two-plate flower   smaller plate   large plate

PRESSED FLOWER PLAQUE

Let the children press pansies or some other flowers several days in advance. After they are well pressed, let the children place them on a paper plate. Cut some cellophane the size of the bottom of the plate. Let child paste cellophane over pressed flowers. Color edge of plate for a frame. Use a bit of ribbon for a hanger and tape to back of plate

HOT PAD OR TRINKET HOLDER

Provide two paper plates, paste, pictures of flowers or any design suitable for kitchen or child's room. Cut one plate in half. Paste flowers on front of uncut plate and on back of the half plate. Color. Turn the half plate upside down and paste flat edges together. Use yarn or ribbon for hanger and paste on back of plate with Scotch tape. This novelty plate hanger will hold several note pads or trinkets.

holder for trinkets

ENVELOPE BOOKMARKS

By cutting the corners of sealed envelopes, little bookmarks may be made that slip over the corners of pages. Colored envelopes add variety to the markers. Children may plan their own cutting designs. Gummed stickers may beautify the markers, too!

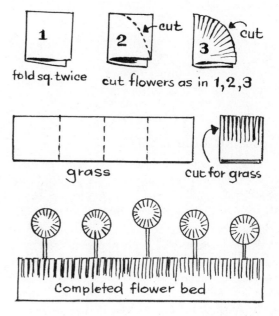

cut flowers as in 1, 2, 3

grass   cut for grass

Completed flower bed

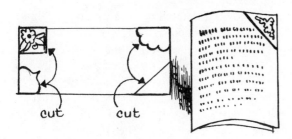

DOILY PLACE MATS

Fold a twelve-inch square piece of paper in half twice. Snip little holes along edges. Fold diagonally and snip some more. The more folds and snipping, the prettier the doily. Paste on oblong piece of colored construction paper. A set of four makes a lovely gift for mother.

Encourage the child to think of others. The giving of a gift can well bear out the teaching of kindness.

PAPER DOILIES

Doily craft is lots of fun and many interesting articles can be created with assorted sizes and styles of paper doilies. Also provide flower seals, paste, greeting card verses and pictures, crayons, white wrapping paper, ribbon or yarn, wax paper.

PLACE MATS

1) GREETING MATS

Use 8 or 10-inch doilies, square or round, with a plain linen-finish center. Select some lovely friendship sentiments or Scripture verses from greeting cards. Cut greeting to fit over center of doily and paste in place. Use

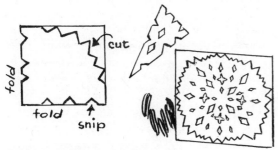

GRASS AND FLOWERS

Provide several 4-inch squares of colored construction paper for each child, in assorted colors. Also provide a stripe of green construction paper 5 inches wide by 24 inches long.

Fold the flower squares twice and cut for flowers, following steps 1, 2, 3. Fold green for grass and cut as noted. Paste grass on strip of wrapping paper (or on wall or window) and add flowers. Cut small strips of green for stems.

2) FLOWER MATS

Choose doilies with flower designs. Children may color several flowers and leaves. A set of 6 small doilies will please mother. She can use them under dessert dishes or on trays when serving punch.

GREETING CARD DOILIES

Let children select and cut out pictures from used birthday greeting cards. Cut out center of small doily (6-inch size is best). Put paste on edge of picture and on inside edge (wrong side, of course) of doily. Place doily on picture and press down all the way around. Use a piece of white wrapping paper (or shelf paper) 10 inches square for envelope. Fold corners to center and place doily inside. Fasten with a flower sticker.

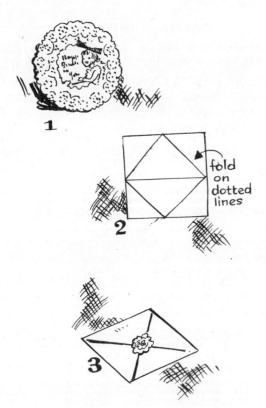

fold
on
dotted
lines

PAPER LACE SACHETS

These sachets make acceptable gifts for mother and grandmother, aunt and sister. While children make these articles, talk about being kind and thoughtful and how nice it is to give love gifts to our families.

1) ROUND SACHET

Choose two matching round doilies about 4 inches in diameter, a bit of cotton or circle of white blotter paper, some sachet or cologne. Color doilies on right side. Place a bit of cotton or a circle of white blotter paper in the center of one of the doilies turned upside down. Sprinkle some sachet powder on the cotton or spray the blotter with cologne. Spread the paste around the edge of the doily and press on the matching doily. Tie a yarn or ribbon bow on the sachet.

2) TRIANGLE SACHET

Use one paper doily, 4 to 6 inches square. Choose a pastel color tissue paper square for a lining. Place doily on the table, wrong side up, and cover with colored tissue paper. Place cotton on one side and spray with cologne or fill with sachet. Fold triangle-wise and paste edges together. Fasten a yarn or ribbon bow to matching corners. This sachet may be hung on a hanger or placed in a drawer.

TRIPLE PICTURE

Select three similar plates in different sizes, paste, ribbon, pictures. Children may paste family snapshots or pictures on the plates. Greeting cards are excellent sources of pictures. Color plates. Place a ribbon hanger on a table and paste the three plates, the largest at the top of the ribbon hanger. Allow several inches of ribbon between each plate.

NOSEGAYS

Color a round 4-inch paper doily. Cut a small hole in the center. Gather a few pansies, sweet peas, sweet-william or other garden flowers and make a little bouquet. Wrap ends of flowers with wax paper and tie with a ribbon or yarn. Slip bouquet through hole in doily. This makes a nice nosegay to wear or to give to a sick friend.

A little bouquet of yarn flowers may be made instead of using real flowers. (See *Yarn Craft.*) Or, gum drop flowers can be made. Place gum drops on ends of fine wire. Wrap wire ends and place in doily. Or, a cluster of lollipops can be used for a nosegay, too! See how many ways you can fix up these nosegays to delight little friends!

TABLE CRUMBER SET

Use one and one-half 9-inch paper plates. Color or decorate one plate as desired. Cut slits for brush on center part of the one-half plate. This makes an excellent gift for mother.

garden flowers

gum drop flowers

yarn flowers

lollypop nosegay

cut

PICTURE FRAME

Use two plain, flat-edge plates. Color the back of one, except the bottom. Cut out bottom and use rim only. Ruffle a strip of crepe paper and paste on edge of uncolored plate. Paste picture in center of plate and paste ribbon hanger on top edge. Paste rim upside down on uncut plate. The ruffle will show between the plate edges as part of the frame. The ribbon hanger will be secure between the plates.

LACE PICTURE

Paste a lace paper doily in the center of a paper plate after coloring it. Color edge of plate and paste picture in the center of doily. Use ribbon for hanger. Punch two holes at top of doily and tie ribbon through holes to form bow.

PAPER STRAWS

DECORATED DRINKING STRAWS

DAISY, CLOWN, KITTY, MR. SUN

Make patterns for drinking straw decorations by folding squares of paper and cutting free-hand as shown in sketches. (Or, you may draw the design before cutting and trace on cardboard to make patterns for children.) Snip or punch holes for inserting straws. Children may draw in detailed designs and color after they trace cardboard pattern. Provide colored cellophane straws and slip designs over straws. Provide fruit nectar or milk in paper cups and have children sip it through straws.

STRAW FLOWERS

Provide each child with eight colored cellophane straws, including two green ones. A bit of Scotch tape, some thread, a piece of construction paper (8½ x 11 inches), paste and a small circle of colored paper will complete the project.

Tie six of the colored straws (no green) tightly in the center. Bend and paste on piece of construction paper so that straws extend above paper. Paste one-half of a circle, about two inches in diameter, over folded center of straws. Fasten green straw for stem to paper with Scotch tape. Cut remaining green straw in thirds for leaves and Scotch tape to stem. Pin flowers to wall for border.

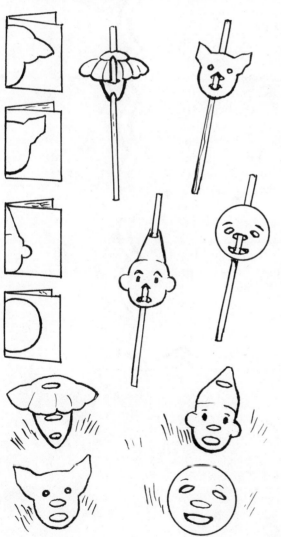

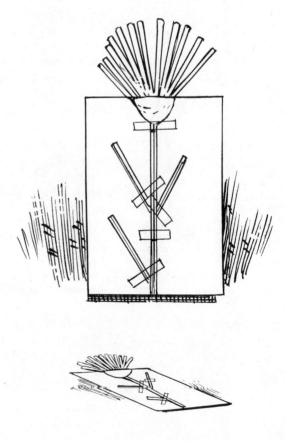

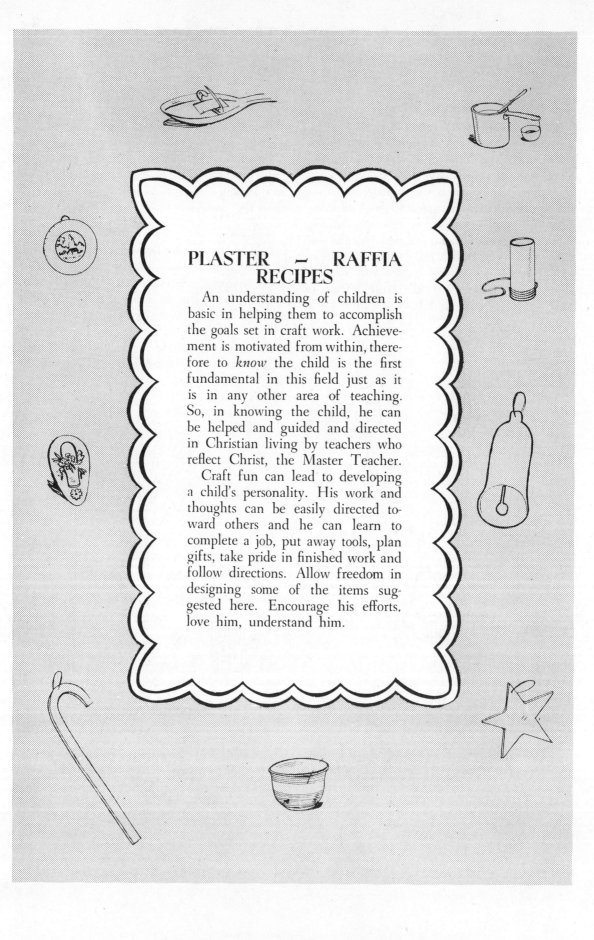

PLASTER — RAFFIA RECIPES

An understanding of children is basic in helping them to accomplish the goals set in craft work. Achievement is motivated from within, therefore to *know* the child is the first fundamental in this field just as it is in any other area of teaching. So, in knowing the child, he can be helped and guided and directed in Christian living by teachers who reflect Christ, the Master Teacher.

Craft fun can lead to developing a child's personality. His work and thoughts can be easily directed toward others and he can learn to complete a job, put away tools, plan gifts, take pride in finished work and follow directions. Allow freedom in designing some of the items suggested here. Encourage his efforts. love him, understand him.

PLASTER CRAFT

Plaster craft offers therapy and fun to little folks who want to make something all by themselves. This craft offers opportunity for considerable ingenuity in designing and should encourage the maker to plan extra gifts for his friends and family.

PLAQUES, PINS

Obtain a supply of patching plaster (or plaster of Paris), some safety pins, adhesive tape, small fluted picnic plates, milk cartons, saucers, colorless nail polish, hairpins, spoons, rubber furniture cups, vaseline and a supply of greeting cards.

1. Select the designs desired for pins or plaques from greeting cards.
2. Prepare molds.
Cut down the empty milk cartons to within 1 inch from the bottom. If spoons, saucers, plates, or rubber furniture cups are used, grease slightly with vaseline.
3. Place picture or design face down and mark with pencil or chalk on the mold, the top of pin or plaque.
4. Mix plaster with water until it will pour, being careful not to make too thin.
5. Pour plaster mix into mold and set in sun.
6. When mixture begins to "set," insert hairpin in top of plaque for hanger. (Yarn or suspension ring hangers will do also.) In making pins insert safety pin in plaster, being careful not to let head fall in too deeply, then place a piece of adhesive tape across pin to prevent it from breaking out later.
7. Allow to dry. When plaster is hard, ease plaque or pin from mold. A slight jarring of the mold will help ease out dried article. The cardboard and rubber molds are better to use since they are flexible.
8. Use emery board and smooth off ends, cover with colorless finger nail polish and allow to dry.
One pound of plaster will make two dozen pins and about six plaques.

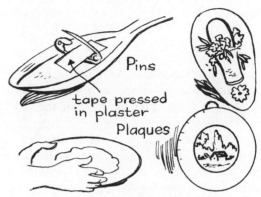

Pins
tape pressed in plaster
Plaques

PAPER RAFFIA CRAFT
(Also see Cans, Bottles and Jars.*)*

JUICE GLASSES
(Use cheese glasses.)

VASES
(Make from bottles.)

SALT AND PEPPER SHAKERS
(Use spice cans.)

BOWLS
(For relishes, bonbons, etc.)

Paper raffia can be made with crepe paper, cut from ¼ to ½ inches wide. Punch a hole in the inside top of a fruit jar lid with a nail. Hammer down the edges or file smooth for children. (Bottle caps make fine twisters, too.) Paper twisters may be purchased at a hobby shop or variety store but the homemade ones will process the paper just as well. Thread crepe paper through the hole and twist as it is pulled through. The pulling and twisting makes tough raffia. Make several balls of raffia in different colors. Paste one end of raffia to bottom of glass, bottle, shakers (cans) or bowl with glue and allow to dry. Wrap raffia round and round until top is reached. Glue and cut. Shellac.

crepe paper
jar lid
raffia
green
yellow
green
bottle vase
glue on bottom
red

RECIPES
(Also see *Finger Paint*)

The following recipes will be helpful in supplying basic materials for use with little folk in craft work. Perhaps some of the older children in your groups can make these supplies and store them for you. Remember, a child learns to do by doing and at the same time he can learn to be very helpful in planning and carrying out a craft program. Be sure that recipes are made in advance so that they may be tested if children have assisted. Proper labeling and storing will assist you in having a smooth-running program.

PASTE

    1 pint cold water
    ¼ pint sifted flour
    1 quart boiling water
    2½ ozs. powdered alum
    1¼ ozs. glycerin
    1 dram oil of wintergreen

Mix a pint of cold water with a half pint of sifted flour and stir thoroughly. Then stir in a quart of boiling water and boil until it thickens, stirring constantly. Let cool. Just before mixture gets cold, stir in 2½ ounces of powdered alum. Next stir in 1½ ounces of glycerin, a little at a time. Finally, mix through it one dram of oil of wintergreen. Put paste in short bottles with straight sides and wide mouths. Keep well capped when not in use.

CORNSTARCH PAINT

    3 tablespoons cornstarch
    1 pint water
    Coloring

Mix 3 level tablespoons of cornstarch with part of a pint of water. Boil remainder of pint, add starch mixture stirring until clear. Remove from stove. After starch paint is cool, add colored paint or other coloring. Use Tintex, vegetable coloring or poster paint for coloring. Store in small bottles.

This paint is excellent for poster painting.

FINGER PAINT

    1 quart water
    3 tablespoons starch
    1 tablespoon flour
    Few drops wintergreen
    Calcimine powder for coloring.

Add a small amount of water to the starch and flour to make a paste. Boil the rest of the water and add the paste. Cook until thick, adding a few drops of oil of wintergreen to keep paint from forming scum. Stir to keep smooth. Add color to suit. Store in jars with tops.

MODELING CLAY

    1 cup flour
    ½ cup salt
    1 teaspoon powdered alum
    Water or glycerin for mixing

Mix thoroughly, then mix with water or glycerin to consistency desired. Color with food coloring.

PAPER PULP CLAY

    Shredded newspapers
    Boiling water
    1 cup flour
    ½ cup salt

Tear newspapers into small pieces and cover with boiling water. Allow to soak for 24 hours. Stir or beat into a pulp. Drain off water and strain pulp through cheesecloth. Add two cups flour and one half cup of salt to each three cups of pulp. Knead like bread dough until the mixture reaches the consistency of putty. Cover with damp cloth.

This clay will be an excellent substitute for modeling clay.

MARBLE PAPER

Wet a piece of tough paper by dipping it in a pan of water. Paint on it large spots or stripes of watercolor. Crumple paper in the hand, squeezing out surplus water. Open and allow to dry. This paper makes fine book covers or mats. Many projects can be made out of this paper in Vacation Bible School.

HECTOGRAPH

12 oz. water
24 oz. glycerin
2 oz. glue, white
2 oz. gelatine or
13 oz. glycerin
Oblong pan, 12 x 7½ inches and about
1½ inches deep

Heat water and white glue in double boiler and keep on fire until melted. Add glycerin and boil one minute. Mix thoroughly and pour the whole mixture into the pan.

CHRISTMAS DECORATIONS

1 cup salt
½ cup cornstarch
½ cup boiling water

Mix dry ingredients thoroughly. Pour boiling water on mixture while stirring vigorously. Keep over fire until mixture forms a dough. Then knead until the mixture reaches the consistency of bread dough. Roll out thin on wax paper. Cut into desired shapes and cover with a moist cloth. (Use Christmas design cookie cutters.) Punch small holes with a nail for attaching strings. Drying takes about 12 hours. If turned two or three times while drying, edges will not curl. When dry, paint on designs. Or, cover with thin film of paste and sprinkle on some glitter. Children will enjoy designing their own ornaments. Tie ribbon strings through holes. Encourage them to pack boxes of designs to send with a small tree to shut-ins, orphanages, etc.

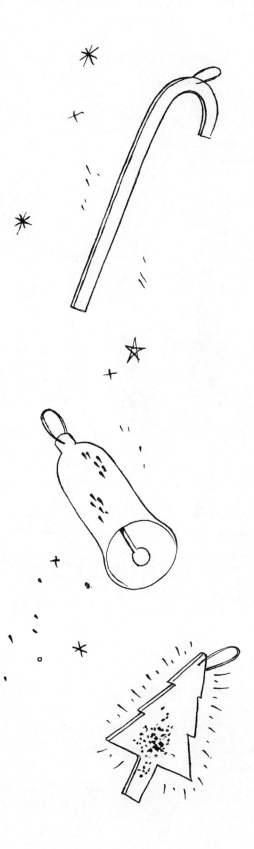

SPOOL CRAFT

"See what I have made!"

How proud and happy the child is with his own handiwork. These simple crafts from spools and scraps can help you, parent and teacher, to help the child achieve. In achieving, there are multiplied opportunities for teaching Christian living. Remind the child of Bible stories of those who shared, of memory verses about being kind, of how we can please God by helping and doing the things that please Him.

A little child who is happily engaged in leisure time will learn to use profitably his time later on. Wholesome competition for achievement and use of time will spur the child on to excel in other activities. So, craft work and an alert teacher will do much to mold today's child into tomorrow's young man or woman.

SPOOL CRAFT
(*Also see* CHRISTMAS.)

Save large spools, small spools, colored spools, all spools. Wash and remove paper. If you wish to color spools for the children, use vegetable food coloring — it is non poisonous.

PANDA BRUSH HOLDER

For each holder provide two spools (medium size), two pieces chenille wire 5 inches long, piece of heavy cardboard, glue.

Use the pattern and trace Panda head on cardboard. Cut out. Place spools in position and mark with pencil through spool holes. Color head. Knot chenille wire on one end for child. Punch holes in cardboard and place knotted wire through spool then through cardboard. Secure spools to cardboard with glue. Fasten wire together at back to form hanging wire. When glue is dry place brush between eyes.

This brush holder may be used in child's closet for clothes brush or for gift for mother and daddy.

OWL BRUSH HOLDER

Follow same procedure as above but make holder from owl head pattern. A circle with two ears will be a simple pattern to follow.

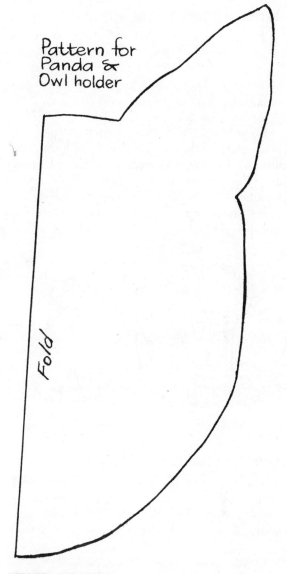

Pattern for Panda & Owl holder

Fold

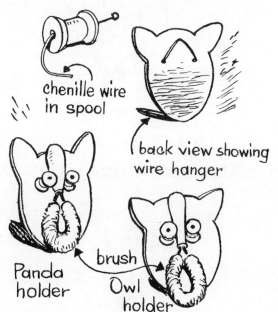

chenille wire in spool

back view showing wire hanger

Panda holder

brush

Owl holder

PENCIL HOLDER

Provide one large spool, eight small spools, piece of cardboard 3½ inches in diameter, glue.

Glue large spool in center of cardboard and glue small spools in circle around large spool. Place pencils in holes of spools. This holder may also be used for crochet hooks, large darning needles, etc. It may be placed on child's desk, on the telephone stand, in the kitchen or in the sewing room.

top view

SPOOL BOUQUET

For each bouquet you will need six pieces of chenille wire about 5 inches long (pipe-cleaners are fine to use), six fancy buttons with large holes, one large spool and one small lace doily.

Color spool as desired. Fasten wires (colored green) through buttons to form the flowers. Double wire stem the depth of spool and place stems in spool holes. Paste spool bouquet on small doily. Use bouquets for party favors, gifts and to decorate trays for sick people.

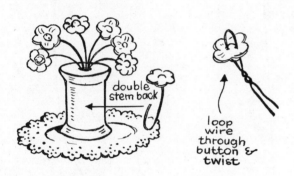

SPOOL GUMDROP TREE

For each tree gather one small branched twig, small assorted gumdrops, one large spool, a name card 2½ by 1 inches and some glue.

Color spool green. Place twig in spool hole. Place gumdrops on tree. Paste spool on card. Write name on card and it will make a lovely place card for any party or a treat for a little sick friend.

SPOOL GAME

This game will give the child many happy hours of fun. Provide one medium size corrugated box, seven large spools, fourteen plain buttons with large holes, seven pieces of chenille wire about five inches long and seven jar rubbers. More than one child can help in making this game.

Obtain a cardboard box and remove ends and flaps (lid). Enlarge clown design and trace on box for children to color. Make small holes where spools will be fastened. Place button on knotted chenille wire, slip wire through spool, then through hole in box and then place a second button on wire and knot. This will make the spool secure and prevent it from coming off box. Tape box together so clown slants. The children may use the jar rubbers and take turns ringing the spools.

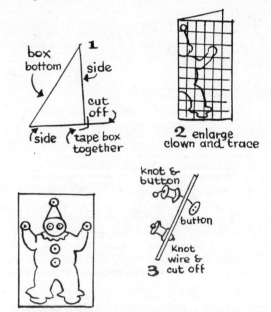

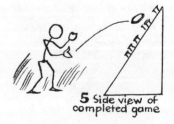

SPOOL ANIMALS

A collection of animals can be made with spools. A few are suggested here but children may design others.

Gather spools, bits of cardboard, cotton, glue, brush bristles, a bit of yarn and ribbon for making these animals.

1) RABBIT

Trace the pattern. Glue front and back to spool as indicated. Paste brush bristles on head for whiskers. Punch hole in back, through spool, and put in ball of cotton for tail. Add ribbon around neck to dress up "Mr. Rabbit."

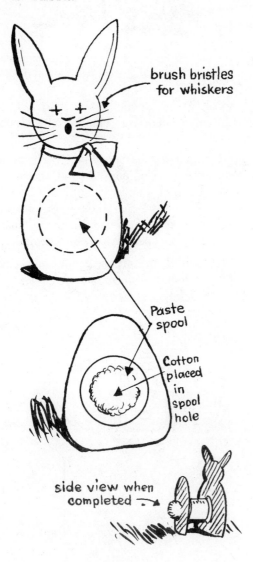

brush bristles for whiskers

Paste spool

Cotton placed in spool hole

side view when completed

2) CAT

Trace the pattern. Glue front and back to spool as indicated. Paste brush bristles on face for whiskers. Punch hole in back through spool and put in string of yarn for tail. If you have a scrap of fur or felt, paste on pattern before gluing to spool. This will give a "touch and feel" effect to animal.

Cat-front

back

spool

yarn

3) DASCHUND DOG

Glue two spools together and allow to dry. Color brown. Trace pattern on light weight cardboard. Cut out. Paste to spools. If you have scrap of suede, paste to pattern for "touch and feel" effect. Paste piece of red felt for tongue.

Trace body for both back and front but draw face on one side only.

side view

SPOOL CANDLE HOLDER AND NUT CUP

Provide one large spool, one piece chenille wire about 5 inches long, one birthday candle, one small nut cup, one card 3 x 1½ inches, one colored flower seal or flower cut from magazine.

Color spool as desired. Paste flower seal or flower design on spool. (Decal is good to use, too.) Color wire and fasten through spool holes to form candle holder handle. Glue spool to card. Glue nut cup to card. Place candle in holder. Write name on card and you are ready for the party!

BLOTTER HOLDER

Cut a square of colored cardboard. Paste gummed album picture corners in each corner. Cut pieces of colored blotter to fit in corners. Glue spool handle to cardboard, on opposite side of where the album picture corners are glued. When one blotter is used up, remove and replace with another.

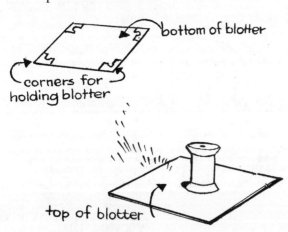

TOP

Provide each child with one large spool, one pencil, a cardboard disc 3 inches in diameter, some glue, a crayon.

Color the cardboard disc and spool (vegetable coloring for spool is best). Glue cardboard disc to spool after making a hole in the center the same size as that in the spool. Insert pencil through disc and spool so that point is opposite from disc. Now, the top is ready to spin!

RING HOLDER

A spool, a short pencil, some yarn and a crayon are needed for making this spool gift.

Insert pencil in the spool hole. Tie some black or brown yarn loops around the spool to make the hair. Draw in a face, or use colored thumbtacks—two blue ones for the eyes and a red one for a mouth. Rings may be placed over the pencil for safe keeping.

Mother will want one near the sink and the family will want one in the bathroom.

SPOOL STRINGS

Gather all sizes of spools, some large colored wooden beads and white shoelaces. Vegetable coloring may be used to color spools if desired.

Remove paper from spools and color. Use the shoelaces for stringing spools. Put large beads in between spools. These strings are welcome gifts in the nursery and home. They are easily cleaned by washing in luke-warm soapy water.

CURTAIN PULLS

Wash spools and let them dry. To dye them, dilute vegetable coloring in cup and dip spools in solution. Use colored yarn and beads to complete pulls. Make a loop of yarn and tie a knot about two inches down. Run ends through a large bead, through the spool, and then through another bead. Wrap some yarn around fingers, slip off and tie through one end and then tie securely to spool. Cut opposite ends of loop for tassel. These pulls make fine Mother's Day gifts.

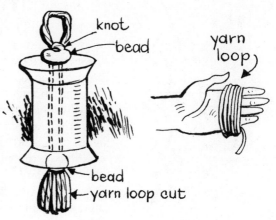

CHRISTMAS ORNAMENTS

String spools as shown in sketches after washing and dipping them in vegetable coloring. Shoelaces, ribbon or yarn are recommended for stringing. A bit of glue on the ends of ribbon and yarn make the stringing easier and may be cut off when ornaments are finished.

TOYS

When a child makes his own toy, his play is much more meaningful. The many steps from craft to play afford golden opportunities for character development. The child follows direction, completes a job, displays his accomplishment, enjoys his creation, and shares his pleasure.

Think of the privilege of guiding little folks and applying principles of Christian teaching. Bible truths can be brought out during the instruction, application can be made during the play time, thoughts can be directed toward others in making extra articles for sick children, gifts, etc.

TOYS
(Also see Paper Bags, Boxes, Games, Spools.*)*

PULL TOY

This toy may be made from a round cereal box. Cut a small hole in each end of the box and run heavy twine through the holes. Allow a little slack in the twine then tie. Seal lid on box with tape after placing a few pebbles or bells inside box. Add another length of twine with spool fastened at end for child to hold when pulling toy. Boxes may be colored or pictures may be pasted on them.

Children may make a supply of these for the Nursery Department of the Sunday school.

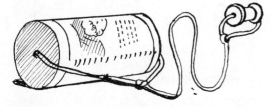

CART

Provide a shoe box, two milk bottle caps (round cardboard style), two brads and some string. If cardboard milk bottle caps are not available, cut wheels from shoe box lid. Cut off long side strips from top of shoe box for cart shafts. Fasten wheels and shafts to sides of box. Tie length of string through holes punched in ends of shafts and pull.

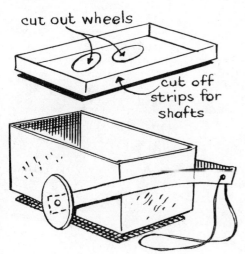

cut out wheels

cut off strips for shafts

HOUSE LIKE JESUS LIVED IN

Provide two boxes with lids for each child, one larger than the other. Help child cut doors in both boxes. Paste on lids. Paste smaller box on top of larger box. Draw stairs with crayon. Cut out trees and flowers from magazines and paste on sides of house. If possible, cut out picture of boy Jesus and paste on cardboard. Cut slit on roof and stand figure in slit.

FLYING BIRDS AND BUTTERFLIES

Provide large pictures of birds and butterflies and let the children mount them on heavy paper then cut them out. Tie a piece of string to a spool and the other end of the string to the bird or butterfly. The child may "fly" the object by holding onto the spool and swinging it in the air. Allow plenty of space for this activity.

Spool

spool

CIRCUS CAR

Provide a cut out of some circus animal (magazines or color books are good sources), a shoe box, eight strips of colored paper ½ inch wide, four brads and four round milk bottle caps.

Child may color box brown for cage. Paste animal in back of cardboard box. Or, mount on cardboard and stand forward in box by pasting on spring hinges to back of box. Fasten milk bottle cap wheels to sides of cage with brads. Fasten a double length of string in center front of cage for handle and tie through a hole punched with scissors and reinforced with Scotch tape. Paste strips of colored paper over opening of box for bars of cage.

spring hinge

JACK IN THE BOX

Provide each child with a strip of paper 11 inches long and 2½ inches wide, a box with lid attached and about 2 inches deep. Cut a head for each child by enlarging pattern as suggested. After child colors head he may paste it to the strip of paper. Fold paper, starting at neck, accordion style, every 2½ inches. Paste the last fold to the bottom

of the box. Tuck head in box, and close lid. Now when child opens box "Mr. Jack" will appear. Child may pull him out then tuck him in.

QUONSET VILLAGE

Save round rolled oats cereal boxes or salt boxes. Let child color these then cut them in half, lengthwise, for him. Give child a piece of corrugated carton and let him color it green for the grass. He then may place the Quonset houses on the green cardboard. Provide strips of white or gray paper and let child paste on cardboard for sidewalks and streets. Flowers may be cut from magazines and pasted against houses for flower beds.

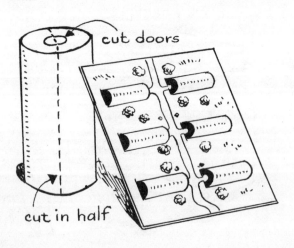

cut doors

cut in half

PLAYING STORE

1) STORE

Gather boxes for shelves: shoe boxes, gift boxes, empty cereal boxes, etc. Paste together. Save small boxes, spice cans, pill boxes, etc., for merchandise.

2) PLAY MONEY AND MONEY BOX

Cut the top from an egg carton box. Save milk bottle caps, linings from small jar and bottle caps, etc. Help child write coin denominations on the discs. Place this "money" in divisions of the egg carton money box. Now the children can go shopping at the "store."

MILK TRUCK

Provide each child with a one-pint milk carton, one half-pint cream carton, four milk bottle tops or round cardboard discs, one piece of cardboard the width of the pint carton and the length of both the pint and one-half pint cartons, paste or glue.

Paste the pint carton on the cardboard with the smaller carton in front for the engine. Paste the cardboard discs to the truck for wheels.

SHELL TURTLE

Materials needed for each turtle are: empty half shell of walnut, piece of construction paper 3 inches square, paste.

Use the pattern given here for the turtle's body and trace on colored construction paper. Glue empty half walnut shell on body.

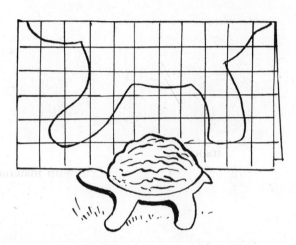

BOX TURTLE

Provide the bottom of a pill or small match box, small wooden spoon, a jar rubber, one brad, some cardboard 1 x 3 inches and some green construction paper 3 inches square.

Trace wooden spoon on cardboard and cut out. Draw eyes on spoon for turtle's head. Cut jar rubber in half and paste on cardboard for turtle's legs. Make a hole in the center of the box and a corresponding hole in the handle of the spoon pattern. Snip openings in box for turtle's head and legs and fasten turtle's body to box with brad. Cut oval from green paper and paste on top of box for turtle's shell. Tie a string around the turtle's neck and when he is pulled watch his legs move!

RHYTHM BAND SHAKERS

Place some small pebbles, or beans, in empty ice cream or cottage cheese cartons. Seal lids on with glue. Color. Use with the drum in the Rhythm Band. Help children shake these in rhythm.

Shakers may also be made by putting a little rice in some empty spice cans. After children color designs on paper it can be pasted around cans.

DRUM

Each child should have one round cereal box, a 27-inch shoestring, some white paper the width of the box, and crayons to make this article.

Child may color the white paper then paste it around the cereal box. Punch a hole in the end of the box and in the lid and help the child thread the shoestring through holes. Tie ends together and glue lid on box. Drum may be worn around neck and played by patting on ends with hands.

WALLPAPER YARN

Children will have to follow carefully given step-by-step directions to make the suggested projects from wallpaper and yarn. Before clear directions can be given, the teacher must know them. Samples of the articles must be made in advance for two reasons: (1) to show completed item and thus stimulate activity; (2) to anticipate any help children may need to complete the project. Take time to repeat directions and be patient with those who are slow to follow.

Throughout this book the use of about-the-house materials will help the children to be conservative with scraps and supplies and to develop ingenuity and creativeness.

WALLPAPER

Gather odds and ends of wallpaper samples from your neighborhood paint and paper store, from your friends, and from about the house. This attractive paper can be used in many ways to make attractive craft items. A few ideas are suggested here. You and the children will think of other projects — do not overlook any good suggestions.

SCRAPBOOKS

Stitch pieces of wallpaper, 16 inches x 10 inches, down the center and let the children make scrapbooks by pasting in pictures from Christmas cards, Sunday school papers, calendars, magazines, etc. These may be wrapped as gifts for children in orphanages, hospitals, missionaries, shut-ins. Wallpaper makes excellent gift wrappings. Projects such as this one will help teach the children thoughtfulness toward others.

PLACE MATS

Save cardboard from tablets, shirts, boxes, etc. Pieces from 8½ inches x 11 inches to 10 inches x 14 inches are good. Cut the wallpaper the same size as the cardboard (with pinking shears) and let the child paste together. Some mats may be bound with colored cellophane tape. Or, rick-rack tape may be pasted on the mat as a border.

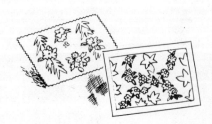

SUNBONNET HAT

Stitch a double thickness of white wrapping paper to a piece of flowered wallpaper size 18 inches x 10 inches. Provide two shoe strings for each hat. Punch three holes on each side of hat, folded width-wise. Lace shoe string from top of fold down and tie in bow. Punch a hole in the two front corners. Cut shoestring in half and tie one piece in each hole. These strings tie under the chin.

WASTEPAPER BASKETS

Gather empty ice cream cartons from drugstores and wash. Popcorn tins may be used also. Cut wallpaper to fit around carton. Let child paste the paper to the carton. If wallpaper is processed with paste on back side, all child has to do is wet it and then fasten it to container. Encourage any ideas the child may have for making the trim especially attractive.

Wastebaskets may be planned for the Sunday school rooms, for gifts and for the home.

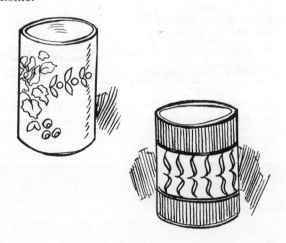

YARN

Empty the yarn basket and gather up all the odds and ends of yarn from friends. Surprise! See what you can make.

NOSEGAYS

Provide a 4-inch paper doily, a fork, scraps of yellow and five other colors of yarn (about 4-foot lengths each), a safety pin.

Cut yellow yarn in 5-inch lengths. Choose an uncut length of yarn in another color. Hold yellow yarn on lower edge of fork and wrap other color around fork until used up.*

* If it is difficult for little people to hold the yellow yarn, they may just wrap the flower around the fork and the teacher may slip a piece of yarn through the loops before the flower is cut.

Tie yellow length in a double knot. Slip scissors along top edge of fork, between loops of yarn, and cut. The yellow will form the center of the flowers. Make five flowers. Hold by yellow yarn and slip through the hole snipped in center of small doily. Attach safety pin for pinning to dress. Trim off excess lengths of yellow yarn. This project makes a lovely nosegay to wear on dress or coat.

yarn around the fingers, held together, and around the small piece of yarn. When yarn is used up, the teacher may tie the small piece into a double knot. Slip yarn off hand.

Tie heavy white crochet thread or thin string around yarn about ¾ inch from top to make a head. Separate eight or ten strands on each side of head for arms. Tie thread about 1½ inches from neck and snip ends. Tie thread about ¾ inch from neck to form waist.

For girl doll just snip ends of yarn to form skirt. For boy doll divide yarn and tie near ends with white thread, then snip. Teacher may braid (or help child do it) some white yarn and attach to girl's head for hair. Make eyes and mouth with three single stitches. A bit of hair can be made for the boy with a few stitches of white thread and a face may be stitched in with three stitches.

Tie the twins together with white yarn fastened from the top of the heads. These dolls may be worn on coat or dress. Little twins are appealing when made in the colors of the races: red, yellow, brown, black and white.

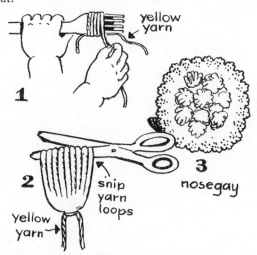

1

yellow yarn

2

yellow yarn

snip yarn loops

3

nosegay

YARN TWINS

Provide about 12 feet of yarn for each doll and let child make two dolls, a boy and a girl. To make the dolls, place a small piece of yarn along index finger and wrap the

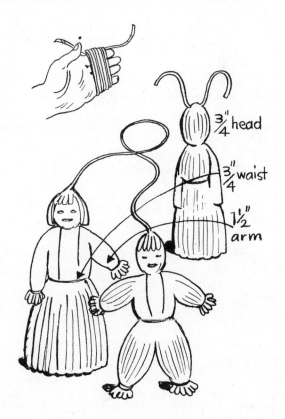

¾" head

¾" waist

1½" arm

My Original Handcraft Ideas

My Original Handcraft Ideas